Thomas Fuller

Joseph's Party-Coloured Coat

A Poem

Thomas Fuller

Joseph's Party-Coloured Coat
A Poem

ISBN/EAN: 9783337006358

Printed in Europe, USA, Canada, Australia, Japan

Cover: Foto ©Thomas Meinert / pixelio.de

More available books at **www.hansebooks.com**

JOSEPH'S PARTY-COLOURED COAT:

A COMMENT ON 1 COR. XI., WITH SEVERAL SERMONS:

AND

DAVID'S HEINOUS SIN,

HEARTY REPENTANCE, HEAVY PUNISHMENT:

A POEM.

BY

THOMAS FULLER, D.D.,
AUTHOR OF THE CHURCH HISTORY OF BRITAIN, ETC., ETC.

EDITED BY
WILLIAM NICHOLS.

LONDON: WILLIAM TEGG.
1867.

JOSEPH'S PARTY-COLOURED COAT:

CONTAINING

A COMMENT

ON PART OF THE ELEVENTH CHAPTER OF THE FIRST EPISTLE
OF ST. PAUL TO THE CORINTHIANS;

TOGETHER WITH SEVERAL SERMONS:

NAMELY,

I. GROWTH IN GRACE.
II. HOW FAR EXAMPLES MAY BE FOLLOWED.
III. AN ILL MATCH WELL BROKEN OFF.
IV. GOOD FROM BAD FRIENDS.
V. A GLASS FOR GLUTTONS.
VI. HOW FAR GRACE MAY BE ENTAILED.
VII. A CHRISTENING SERMON.
VIII. FACTION CONFUTED.

By T. F.

JOHN vi. 12.
"GATHER up the fragments that remain, that nothing be lost."

LONDON:
PRINTED BY JOHN DAWSON, FOR JOHN WILLIAMS;
AND ARE TO BE SOLD AT HIS SHOP, AT THE SIGN OF THE CRANE, IN PAUL'S
CHURCH YARD.
1640.

TO

THE RIGHT WORSHIPFUL THE LADY JANE COVERT,

OF PEPPER HARROW, IN SURREY.

MADAM,

Custom hath made it not only pardonable, but necessary, to flatter in Dedicatory Epistles. Epitaphs and Dedications are credited alike.

But I will not follow the stream herein: First, because I account it beneath my calling to speak any thing above the truth. Secondly, because of you it is needless. Let deformed faces be beholden to the painter; Art hath nothing to do, where Nature hath prevented it.

Wherefore I will turn my praising of you into prayer for you; desiring God to strengthen and increase all goodness in you, and give you perseverance,—that golden clasp, which joins grace and glory together.

Thus desiring to shroud my weak labours under your favourable patronage, I rest

Your Ladyship's in all service,

T. F.

EDITOR'S PREFACE.

This volume contains two of Fuller's earliest and scarcest works. The Poem, indeed, " David's Heinous Sin," &c., seems to have been his very *first* venture in the market of letters; being published in 1631, when he was only in his twenty-third year. Though, as might be expected, parts of it are rather juvenile in style and matter, yet it is well worth preserving, containing as it does many bright thoughts and quaint phrases; and bearing promise of the genuine and ready wit which afterwards gave to the name of Thomas Fuller an individuality as distinguished as that of Thomas Hood in our own age.

" Joseph's Party-coloured Coat " was published in 1640, and, as will be seen, is replete with valuable matter clothed in a lively style.

Whilst modernizing the spelling, I have not thought it right to follow the example of some editors in reducing every quotation from Scripture to a conformity with our present Authorized Version:—a process which often obliterates the *point* of an old author's sentence, and which appears to be carried out in ignorance both that there ever was any other English version besides the one now universally current, and that many divines of former days were in the habit of giving their own rendering of the original.

WILLIAM NICHOLS.

6, *Stratheden Villas, Hackney,*
1867.

CONTENTS.

JOSEPH'S PARTY-COLOURED COAT.

	PAGE
COMMENT ON 1 CORINTHIANS XI	5
GROWTH IN GRACE	99
HOW FAR EXAMPLES ARE TO BE FOLLOWED	112
AN ILL MATCH WELL BROKEN OFF	125
GOOD FROM BAD FRIENDS	137
A GLASS FOR GLUTTONS	146
HOW FAR GRACE CAN BE ENTAILED	158
A CHRISTENING SERMON	168
FACTION CONFUTED	184

DAVID'S HEINOUS SIN 199
DAVID'S HEARTY REPENTANCE 219
DAVID'S HEAVY PUNISHMENT 228

A COMMENT

ON 1 COR. XI. 18, &c.

VERSE 18.

For first of all, when you come together in the church, I hear there be divisions among you; and I partly believe it.

THE apostle calleth the Corinthians to an account, and readeth his black bill unto them. It containeth several *items*, which you may read in the following chapters; but the *imprimis* is in the text: "For first of all," &c.

When you come together in the church, &c.

OBSERVATION.

Even in the non-age and infancy of Christianity, there were churches appointed for God's holy service. True, some take "church" here *pro cœtu fidelium;* yet Theophylact, and all Greek writers generally, expound it, "the material place of meeting."

Two things then were chiefly aimed at in churches:

1. Receipt; that the place were capable to contain the people.
2. Privacy.

Being then under persecution, they built not their churches to be seen, but not to be seen; and then were as plain in their houses as in their dealing. Beauty and magnificence were of later date in Christian temples, when religion grew acquainted with peace and prosperity. And good reason God's house now should be decently garnished. Some, shunning whorish gaudiness, leave the church to sluttish nastiness; the font (our Jordan) having more mud than water in it; the communion-table unseemingly kept.

CAUTION.

Withal let us take heed lest, as it hath been observed in England, that great house-building hath been the bane of good house-keeping; so let us take heed lest piety in us be so much the worse, by how much our churches are better than they were in the time of St. Paul. What a shame would it be, if there should be more light in the church windows than in our understanding, more pious sentences written in their walls than in our hearts, more uniformity in the building than in our behaviours!

I hear there be divisions among you.

QUESTION.

How came St. Paul by this intelligence? Was not he at Philippi, when he wrote this Epistle, (as appears by the postscript,) which was many miles from Corinth? How heard the apostle of these divisions at such a distance?

ANSWER.

St. Paul was cunning in a kind of Christian and lawful magic. All the world was his circle; (for so he saith of himself, "The care of all churches lieth upon me," 2 Cor. xi. 28;) and some faithful friends in every church were his familiar spirits in this circle, to inform him of all considerable passages. So that St. Paul was at Corinth, when he was not at Corinth; absent in person, present by his proxies, these intelligencers which kept correspondency with him.

DOCTRINE.

Men in authority have quick ears to hear at a great distance. The mutterings of malefactors are hallooings to magistrates, who hear distinctly what offenders but whisper to themselves.

USE.

Let none therefore be encouraged to sin through a confidence to be concealed. What though sinners be the servants of the prince of darkness, and therefore hope to obtain from their lord and master a protection, that no punishment may arrest them? yet let them know, that though the place wherein they sin seem to them as dark as Egypt, it is as light to men in authority as the land of Goshen. Lions sleep with their eyes open; magistrates, with their eyes both open and seeing: when we think them blind, they behold: when deaf, with St. Paul they " hear."

QUESTION.

Did these men (whosoever they were) well in telling St. Paul these discords of the Corinthians? Had they not better have gone backward, and covered the nakedness of their neighbours with the cloak of silence? Pity it is but that his tongue should be for ever bound to the peace, who will prate of every fault he finds in another; and at the best they are but clacks and tell-tales for their pains.

ANSWER.

Had they told it to some scoffing Ham, or mocking Ishmael, who would have made music to himself of the Corinthians' discords, then they had been faulty in relating the faults of others. "Tell it not in Gath, nor publish it in Askelon; lest the," &c. (2 Sam. i. 20.) But it being told to St. Paul, who would not mock, but bemoan— not defame, but reform—these offenders, it was no breach, but a deed of charity, and the doers hereof benefactors herein to the church of Corinth.

DOCTRINE.

It is both lawful and laudable to discover the faults of our dearest friends, to those who have power and place to reform them. Thus Joseph brought to his father Jacob the evil deeds of his brethren. (Gen. xxxvii. 2.) Indeed, the devil is called " the accuser of the brethren ; " (Rev. xii. 10;) but he accuseth them often without cause, even without charity, who, since he hath been cast into hell, knows no other heaven than to do mischief. But for a man to open the sins, the wounds of his neighbour, not with desire to put him to torment, but that the chirurgeon [surgeon] may search and salve them, is an action most charitable.

There are divisions.

OBJECTION.

But did not St. Paul, in the second verse of this chapter, praise the Corinthians ? " Now I commend you, brethren, that you remember me in all things, and keep the ordinances, as I delivered them to you." Were they grown so bad since the beginning of this chapter ? or doth St. Paul with St. Augustine write a retractation of what he had written before ? Is this fair dealing, that he who formerly had by his commendations given the Corinthians a general acquittance from all their faults, should now come over them with an after-reckoning, and charge them with the sin of divisions?

ANSWER.

1. Some answer, *Omnia, id est, pleraque omnia.** So that "all the ordinances" are to be expounded "the greatest part of them."

2. Others by "ordinances" understand only certain ecclesiastical rites and ceremonies, † touching the discipline of the church, which had no necessary influence either on doctrine or manners; so that the Corinthians might be observant of all these, and yet peccant both in life and belief.

If this be the meaning, then let us take heed that, though we be whole in discipline, we be not halting in doctrine; though sound in ceremonies, not sick in manners; there being no such inseparable connexion betwixt the one and the other, but that a man may observe all orders in church service, and yet be disorderly in his life and conversation. Lightning ofttimes breaks the sword, yet bruises not the scabbard; so error and viciousness may break all piety and religion in us, though in the mean time the sheath of religion (formal decency and outward conformity) remain in us sound and entire.

Calvin's opinion is that the apostle, commend-

* Cornel. à Lapide on the text.
† Thom. Morton in his comment upon 1 Cor. xi.

ing the Corinthians, meaneth the main and general body of the church, though there might be many stragglers justly to be reproved; confessing *laborasse quidem alios aliis vitiis: interea tamen ab universo corpore retentam fuisse formam quam commendaverat.** That church therefore is, and is to be counted and commended for, a good church, whose head is whole, heart healthful, all vital parts entire, though having a lame leg, a bleared eye, a withered hand, some bad and vicious members, belonging unto it.

And I partly believe it.

That is, I believe some of you are guilty of this fault, though others be innocent.

DOCTRINE.

General censures, condemning whole churches, are altogether uncharitable. Angle out the offenders by themselves, but take heed of killing all with a drag-net: and grant many, yea, most to be faulty, yet some may be guiltless. Wickedness was not so general a rule in Sodom but that righteous Lot was an exception from it. See Obadiah (as a jewel in the head of a toad) steward of Ahab's wicked household. Yea, seeing impiety intrudes itself amongst the thickest of God's saints, (even drowning Ham in Noah's ark,) just

* Calvin on 1 Cor. xi. 2.

it is that God should have some names even where the throne of Satan is erected.

Let us therefore follow the wary proceedings of Jehu, (2 Kings x. 23,) who, being about to kill Baal's priests, caused a strict search before to be made: "Search, and look that there be here with you none of the servants of the Lord, but the servants of Baal only." So, when we are about with censuring to murder the credits of many together, let us take heed that there be not some orthodox amongst those whom we condemn all to be heretics; some that desire to be peaceable in this our Israel, amongst those whom we condemn for all factious schismatics.

But these words, "I partly believe it," may thus also be expounded, as well of the faults as of the persons; as if he had said, "I believe these accusations only in part, and hope they are not so bad as they are reported."

DOCTRINE.

When fames are brought unto us from good hands, let us not be so incredulous as to believe no part of them; nor so uncharitable as to believe all; but with St. Paul "partly believe it." The good man carrieth a Court of Chancery in his own bosom, to mitigate the rigour of common reports with equal and favourable interpretations.

REASON I.

Because Fame often creates something of nothing, always makes a great deal of a little. 'T is true of Fame what is said of the devil: it has been "a liar from the beginning;" yea, and sometimes a murderer. Absalom slew one of David's sons, and Fame killed all the rest. (2 Sam. xiii. 30.)

REASON II.

Because men in reporting things often mingle their own interests and engagements with their relations, making them better, or worse, as they themselves stand affected. Water resembleth both the taste and colour of that earth through which it runneth; so reports relish of their relators, and have a blush and a smack of their partial dispositions; and therefore such relations are not to be believed in their full latitude, extent, and dimension.

IT CONFUTES

1. Those that will believe nothing of what they hear reported, though warranted by never so good witnesses. Though they be persuaded, they will not be persuaded, and will not credit any accusations, though never so just; yea, sometimes are so far from trusting the tongues of others, that they will not trust their own eyes. I bear them witness, these men have charity, but not according to knowledge.

2. But where *too much* charity hath slain her thousands, *too little* hath slain her ten thousands.

More men there be who take all reports upon the credit of the relators, and never weigh them in the scales of their own judgments, to see if they be too light or no. Yea, some are so excessive in this kind, their belief outstretcheth the report: what is told them to be done out of ignorance, they believe to be out of knowledge; what is told them to be done out of infirmity, they believe to be done out of presumption. They need not say with the man in the Gospel, "Lord, I believe, help my unbelief;" but, "Lord, pardon my too much belief, pardon my over-credulity; in that I believe all, and more than all, reported."

To conclude : let not our beliefs be altogether of clay, to receive any impression; nor altogether of iron, to receive none at all. But as the toes in the image of Nebuchadnezzar's dream were partly iron and partly clay, so let our beliefs be composed of charity, mixed with our credulity; that, when a crime is reported, we may with St. Paul "partly believe it."

VERSE 19.

For there must be also heresies among you, that they which are approved may be made manifest among you.

Here St. Paul argueth *à minore ad majus;* being the more easily induced to believe there might be divisions among them, because also there must be heresies.

DOCTRINE.

Heresies are worse than schisms, false doctrines more dangerous than divisions. The former sins against faith; the latter, against charity; and though these two graces be sisters and twins, yet faith is the eldest and choicest.

However, as children use to say, they love father and mother both best; so let us hate heresies and schisms both worst. The rather because schism is a fit stock to graft heresy on; yea, of their own accord, old schismatics, ripened with age, grow young heretics. Witness the Donatists, who, as St. Augustine saith,* were but pure schismatics at first, and turned heretics afterwards.

QUESTION.

What is a heresy? A demand very important to be answered, seeing St. Paul saith, "After the way which they call heresy, so worship I the God of my fathers." (Acts xxiv. 14.)

ANSWER.

Heresy is an error in the fundamentals of religion, maintained with obstinacy. It must be in the fundamentals. In the primitive church many were too lavish in bestowing the name of "heretic" on those which dissented from the

---

* *Libro de Hæresibus ad Quod vult Deum.*

church in (as I may say) venial errors. A charitable man would have been loath to have been of the jury, to condemn Jovinian for a heretic, on no other evidence than that he maintained marriage in merit to be equal with virginity. As, therefore, by those many kings mentioned in the Old Testament, "thirty and one" in the little land of Canaan, (Joshua xii. 24,) is meant only toparchs, not great kings, but lords of a little dition * and dominion; so in the ancient catalogues of heretics, (especially of that which Philaster made,) † we may understand in some of them only erroneous persons, swerving from the truth.

The next thing necessary in a heresy is, that it be maintained with obstinacy; which is the dead flesh, making the green wound of an error fester into the old sore of a heresy. Those two hundred men of Jerusalem, (2 Sam. xv. 11,) who followed Absalom to Hebron "in their simplicity," and "knew not any thing," cannot properly be counted traitors or rebels: no more can people purely erroneous, who do not bolt and bar their eyes against the beams of truth, but willingly would embrace it, if delivered unto them, and maintain an error out of conscience, not knowing

* [Lordship, or dominion :—a word rarely used in Fuller's day, and now quite obsolete.—ED.]

† St. Augustine, *loco priùs citato*, saith of him, *Hæreses quidem ipse commemorat, sed mihi appellandæ hæreses non videntur.*

the truth, be accounted heretics. Charitable therefore was the cautiousness of Epiphanius, who would not condemn the Anthropomorphites for heretics, (who, mistaking some places of Scripture, which speak of God's eyes, feet, and hands, conceived Him to be of a bodily substance,) but rather imputed it to their simplicity than obstinacy,—*rusticitati eorum tribuens*.

QUESTION.

Whether doth every heretic maintain that which in his own conscience he knows to be false?

ANSWER.

No: perchance some heretics at first may strive to defend errors, even against the reluctancies of their own judgments; and God may afterwards justly take from them that light which they thrust from themselves: and as great liars tell lies so long till at last they themselves believe them to be true, so many heretics so long maintain falsehoods against their judgment, till at last, being delivered up to a reprobate mind, they believe their very errors to be truth.

And we will take just occasion to describe those qualities which dispose a man to be a father and founder of a heresy.

1. He must be abominably proud. Pride is the key of the work, especially spiritual pride. When one is elated with conceited sanctity above others, chiefly he will snarl at his superiors, and quarrel

with men in authority, that those are before him in place, which are behind him in piety. 2. To pride add discontentment, that his preferments bear not proportion to his supposed deserts. Thus Arius would be an Arian, because he could not be a bishop. 3. Learning void of humility. "The serpent was the subtilest of all the beasts in the field." (Gen. iii. 1.) In this kind a dunce is no dish for the devil's tooth. But, in default of learning, good natural parts will serve the turn, especially memory (which is $θαυματουργός$, a "wonder-working" faculty) and a fluent expression; so that, when he calleth for words, "Gad:" behold, "a troop cometh." If both learning and natural parts be wanting, yet (as, when the golden shields were taken away, Rehoboam's brasen shields did the deed, and made as much glittering, 2 Chron. xii. 10) boldness and brasen-faced impudence will supply the place, especially if he trades with the vulgar, broaches dregs, and founds a dull and sottish heresy, which hath no affinity with learning. To varnish all these, there must be pretended piety and austerity of life; and how foul or filthy soever the postern or back-door be, the door which opens to the street must be swept and garnished. Put all these together,—pride, discontent, learning, (at least-wise good parts, or impudency,) pretended sanctity; and they spell together *hæresiarcham*, one cut and carved out to be "ringleader and captain of a heresy."

To prevent these mischiefs, let such men pray to God for humility, (that virtue which is most worth, yet costeth the least to keep it,) and beware of spiritual pride, which is the hectic fever of the soul, feeding on the very moisture of the heart of piety. Let them beware of discontentment, which is a direct quarrelling with God, who is the Fountain of all preferment, though men may be the channel; and he who hath the least from Him, hath more than He deserveth. And grant preferment is denied thee, be not so childish to cast away a crown, because thou canst not get a counter; willingly throw away thy soul, and foolishly revenge the fault of the times, as thou countest it, upon thyself. Lastly, if God hath bestowed good parts upon thee, pray to Him to sanctify them to thee: otherwise the greatest memory may soon forget itself, and a fluent tongue may cut his throat that hath it.

So much for the character of an arch-heretic. But those whose barren wits want pregnancy to be the mothers of heresies, may notwithstanding serve for dry nurses to feed and foster them; and to this purpose the devil will make use of them.

A plain follower of a heresy may be thus described. First, he must be ignorant; for he that knows nothing will believe any thing. These be maidens for their religion; and therefore the opinion which first woed them, first wins them; first come, first served. Old seducers, as it is 2 Tim. iii. 6, "creep into houses, and lead captive silly women laden with sins, led away with divers lusts, ever learning, and never able to come to the knowledge of the truth." Secondly, desirous of novelty. It is an old humour for men to love new things; and in this point even many barbarians are Athenians. Lastly, (what resulteth from the two former,) they must have the persons of men in much admiration, doting on some fancied man's parts and perfections, and entertaining any thing he saith, because he said it.

To prevent these mischiefs, that men may not be followers of heresies, let the meanest-parted labour to attain to some competent measure of knowledge in matters of salvation, that so he may not trust every spirit, but be able to try whether he be of God, or no. Believe no man with implicit faith in matters of such moment; for he who buys a jewel in a case, without ever looking on it, deserves to be cozened with a Bristol stone, instead of a diamond. Secondly, kill the itch of novelty in thy soul, practising the prophet's precept, Jer. vi. 16: "Thus saith the Lord, Stand ye in the ways, and see, and ask for the old paths, where is the good way, and walk therein, and ye shall find rest for your souls." Lastly, love and admire no man's doctrine for his person, but rather love his person for his doctrine.

And now to return to the very words of the text.

There must be also heresies.

There is a double " must," or a twofold necessity of things being. First, an absolute necessity; when the thing hath in itself the cause of its necessary being. Thus God alone *must be ;* (for what can be, if Being itself be not?) and must be good, and must be true. Secondly, a conditionate " must," or a necessity *ex hypothesi*, which must needs be if such a thing be granted before. As, suppose the sun be risen, and it must be day. Such a conditionate necessity is this in the text: for upon the pre-supposition of these two things, which cannot be denied,—that the devil goeth about like a roaring lion, seeking whom he may devour, and that the flesh lusteth against the spirit, making men prone to all wickedness; hence it followeth there must be heresies. Thus he that beholdeth a family, and findeth the master to be careless, the mistress negligent, the sons riotous, the servants unfaithful; he may safely conclude that family cannot be safe, but must be ruined. "There must be heresies;" parallel to that, Luke xvii. 1, "It is impossible but that offences should come." But far be it from us to conceive that God imposeth a fatal necessity, or by the irresistibleness of His decree urgeth or enforceth any to be heretics. Their badness He wisely permits, but in no wise is the cause or author thereof.

Among you.

You Corinthians, though men of excellent parts and endowments, are not privileged from having heresies among you; yea, happily, because of your excellent natural gifts, are more disposed thereunto. Or take it generally, "among you" Christians; for properly heresies have their rise and original out of the church, and issue thence, according to the 1 John ii. 19, "They went out from us, but they were not of us; for if they had," &c. I see not therefore how Epiphanius can well make Platonists and Pythagoreans to be heretics, (the latter for their opinion of transanimation,) seeing neither of these were ever of the church.

That they which are approved may be made manifest among you.

That they whom God from all eternity in His secret counsel hath approved, may have their Epiphany and manifestation unto the world; that, thus discovered, they may receive from men a testimonial of their soundness and sincerity. Not that God hereby gaineth any accession of knowledge: ("Fore-known unto God are all His works from the beginning of the world," Acts xv. 18:), but others hereby are certified and assured of that which was doubtful before. Thus oftentimes goldsmiths, though they themselves be sufficiently satisfied of the goodness of the gold, yet " put it to the touch," to content the beholders.

And hereby also those which are not approved are made manifest. Many who do εὐπροσωπῆσαι ἐν σαρκί, " make a brave show in the flesh," and carry it in a high triumphant way, will prove but base when brought to the trial; whilst many unknown men, of whom the world took no notice, not suspected for any worth, shall acquit themselves valiant, and appear glorious to God and all good men. Many a bright candle, formerly hid under a bushel, of a private and obscure life, shall then be set on a candlestick, and shine forth to the world; and shall cause,

1. Glory to God, who shall be honoured and praised in these His servants; and, as it is Matthew ix. 8, "the multitudes" will "marvel, and glorify God, which hath given such power unto men."

2. Honour to these His champions of the truth. Never had Athanasius so answered his name, and been so truly "immortal" in his memory, but for opposing of the Arians. Never had St. Augustine been so famous, but for quelling of Manicheans, Pelagians, Donatists, and whom not? for all his heretics lay pat for his hand to dash them in pieces.

3. Clearing to the truth. Her old evidences, which have lain long neglected, will then be searched and found out; her rusty arguments will be scoured over and furbished up. "Many will run to and fro, and knowledge shall be increased." Those which, before shooting at the truth, were over, under, or wide, will now, with the left-handed Gibeonites, hit the mark at a hair's breadth, and fail not. Many parts of true doctrine have been but slenderly guarded, till once they were assaulted by heretics; and many good authors in those points which were never opposed, have written but loosely, and suffered unwary passages to fall from their posting pens. But when thieves are about the country, every one will ride with his sword, and stand on his guard: when heretics are abroad in the world, writers weigh each word, ponder each phrase, that they may give the enemies no advantage.

4. Confirmation to weak Christians. Many, whose hearts and affections were loyal to the truth, but likely to be overborne by the violence of the opposite party, will hereby be strengthened, and established in the right.

5. Those will be reduced, who (as Agrippa said of himself, Acts xxvi. 28, that he was "almost a Christian") are almost heretics, not as yet *formati et radicati hæretici;* but such as, well going, or rather ill going, that way, will pluck one foot out

of the snare, and will return to the bosom of the church.

6. Lastly, the hardened will be made unexcusable, who obstinately persist in their errors. They cannot plead they lost their way for want of guides, but for mere wilfulness. And thus God is so good, He would suffer no heretics to be in the world, were He not also so strong and so wise that He can extract thus many goods by permitting them.

VERSES 20, 21.

When you come together therefore into one place, this is not to eat the Lord's supper.
For in eating every one taketh before other his own supper: and one is hungry, and another is drunken.

Of the sense of the first of these verses are many and different opinions, both what is meant by "This is not to eat," and "the Lord's supper." Omitting variety of interpretations, we will embrace that which we conceive the best.

This is not to eat the Lord's supper.

As if he had said: "True it is, ye Corinthians, when ye come together to one place, you eat the Lord's supper;" (meaning the body and blood of Christ in the sacrament, so expounded by St. Augustine*

* *Epist.* cxxviii. *ad Januar.,* cap. 5. *Ipsam acceptionem Eucharistiæ cænam Dominicam vocat.*

and Ambrose, with many other Latin writers;) "and yet, though you eat it, you do not eat it. You perform the material part of the action, but leave out the life and soul thereof, not doing it legally and solemnly according to Christ's institution. Such is your want of charity, and excess of riot, in your love-feasts, (which you eat before the sacrament,) whereby your souls are disturbed, distempered, and quite put out of tune to eat the supper of the Lord, as ye ought."

DOCTRINE.

A duty not done as it ought to be done, is in effect not done at all. Isaiah lxiv. 7: "There is none that calleth upon Thy name, that stirreth up himself to take hold of Thee." Not that the true church of God, in whose person it is spoken, (as antiquity expounds it, and may be demonstrated by unanswerable arguments,) do any times wholly neglect, though too often negligently perform, their calling on God. Not doing it with that faith and constancy, care and fervency, devotion and diligence, as they ought, and God requires; they did not call on God, in the same sense as St. Paul speaketh, "This is not to eat."

USE.

It will abate their pride, who rest on *opus operatum*, as bad divinity as Latin. For "a deed done" is a deed not done, where the manner of the doing confutes and confounds the matter of the deed. Yea, in the best of God's children,—as Gideon's army of two-and-thirty thousand did shrink to three hundred, (Judges vii. 6,)—so it is to be feared that their so many sermons heard, prayers made, alms given, which they score up to themselves and reckon upon, will shrink in the tale, when God takes account of them; and prove sermons not heard, prayers not made, alms not given, because not done in form as He requires.

Yet it is some comfort unto us, if all our actions proceed from faith, and aiming at God's glory; so that the failings be rather in the branches and leaves than in the roots of our performances. As for the unregenerate, they so remaining have in them *læsum principium* of all true pious works; all their Divine actions are none at all; it being true of their whole list, what one* writes of the year of our Lord 903, *Annus suâ tantùm obscuritate illustris,* "famous only for this, that nothing famous was done in it," and the whole story thereof a very blank.

For in eating every one taketh before other his own supper.

Herein the apostle reproveth their abuses in their love-feasts; whose institution, declination, and corruption, we will briefly describe.

THEIR INSTITUTION.

Love-feasts were founded on no express com-

* Spondanus, *Annal. Eccles., in anno* 903.

mand in Holy Writ, but only on the custom of the church, who immediately before the receiving of the sacrament, as appears both by the text and St. Augustine's* comment on it, (though St. Chrysostom makes these love-feasts to be after the taking of the eucharist,) used to have a great feast, to which all the poor people were invited, on the charges of the rich. This they did partly in imitation of our Saviour, who instituted the sacrament after a full supper; and partly in expression of their perfect love and charity towards all men.

THEIR DECLINATION.

But the number of rich men increased not proportionably with the poor. 1 Cor. i. 26: "Behold your calling, that not many wise men after the flesh, not many mighty, not many noble, are called." The church, in time of persecution especially, is like a copse, wherein the underwood grows much thicker and faster than the oaks. Hence came it to pass, that there were few hosts, many guests; few inviters, many to be invited; and the burden growing heavy, lying on few backs, they wholly omitted the poor, who, loath to come without any invitation,—the warrant to keep a guest from trespassing on good manners, —were excluded from their feasts.

* *Loco priùs citato.*

THEIR CORRUPTION.

Thus love to men in want was quickly turned into want of love; *Mare Euxinum*, into *Mare Axinum*;* love-feasts, into no-love-feasts. (Thus too often charity is changed into bargaining; hospitals turned into exchanges, wherein those are taken in, that can give; and those left out, that have nothing.) The poor people in Corinth did see, and smell, what the rich men tasted; *Tantalizing* † all the while, and having their penury doubled by the *antiperistasis* of others' plenty; yea, riot and excess; for some of them were drunken.

Yet mark by the way, that St. Paul doth not plant his arguments point-blank to beat these love-feasts down to the ground, wholly to abrogate and make a nullity of them, but only to correct and reform the abuses therein, that there might be less riot in the rich, and more charity towards the poor.

USE.

Let not things simply good in themselves, be done away for their abuses. Abraham said unto God,

* ["The Euxine," or "Hospitable," "Sea" into "the Inhospitable Sea;" the latter having once been its designation, according to Ovid, who evidently thought the epithet very appropriate :—

Frigida me cohibent Euxini litora Ponti:
Dictus ab antiquis Axenus ille fu't.
Trist., iv., el. iv., 55.—ED.]

† [That is, suffering like Tantalus.—ED.]

"To slay the righteous with the wicked, that be far from Thee;" (Gen. xviii. 25;) and far be it from us to cashier the good use of a thing, with the ill abuses annexed thereunto. He is a bad husband that, having a spot in his coat, will cut out the cloth, not wash out the dirt. Wherefore, in matters of a mixed nature, wherein good and bad are confusedly jumbled together, let us with the fire of judgment try the dross from the gold, and with the fan of discretion winnow the chaff from the corn.

For in eating every one taketh, &c.

By "every one," understand not every particular person in the church of Corinth,—for then how could some be "hungry?"—but every division; the faction of Paul apart, of Apollos apart, the sect of Cephas by itself.

His own supper.

Meaning that love-feast, or plentiful supper, whereof formerly; therefore called their "own," both because severally provided for their own faction, as also in distinction of the Lord's supper, which they took afterwards.

And one is hungry.

Here is nothing in the poor to be condemned. For, that they were hungry, was no sin in them, but their punishment; God's pleasure, and the rich men's fault.

OBSERVATION.

Poverty sometimes keeps men innocent, whiles abused wealth makes rich men to offend.

Something is here in the poor to be commended, that they would be "hungry." Our age affords such unmannerly harpies, they would have snatched the meat out of the rich men's mouths. Some will not want a fire, if there be fuel in their neighbour's yard. But, O, let us not unlawfully remove the landmark of our estates. Let us rather trespass against modesty than honesty; go naked, than steal clothes; be hungry, and fast, than feast on forbidden food.

And another is drunken.

QUESTION.

Is it credible that any of the Corinthians, being about to receive the sacrament, would be so far overtaken as to be "drunken?"

ANSWER.

Surely not so drunken as he, Proverbs xxiii. 35: "They have stricken me," said he, "and I was not sick; they have beaten me, and I felt it not." They pronounced not "Sibboleth" for "Shibboleth;" so that it might have been said to them, as it was to St. Peter, "Thy very language betrayeth thee." Sure their tongues, eyes, and feet, were loyal enough to preserve their masters' credit. So then by "drunken" here understand the highest flight and pitch of mirth. And as herbs hot in the fourth degree are poison, so *summa hilaritas* is *ima ebrietas*, "the highest stair of mirth is the lowest step of drunkenness."

DOCTRINE.

There is a concealed drunkenness, which no informer can accuse, no witness can testify, no earthly judge can punish; yet is it liable to a censure in the Court of Heaven, and counted drunkenness in the eyes of God. And though others cannot perceive it in us, we may take notice of it in ourselves, especially if we examine ourselves,—1. By our unaptness to serve God in our general or particular callings. 2. By the quantity of the liquor we have drunk. 3. By the company with whom we drink. For as some who of themselves never take notice of their own fast going, yet are sensible of it when they hear some of their company, whose legs are not so long and so strong, begin to complain; so, though of ourselves we find no alteration in our own temper, yet if any of our companions in drinking, who started from the same place and ran the same pace with us, begin to be tired, let them be our monitors, that [it] is high time *claudere jam rivos*, to leave off our course, as being already drunkenness before God.

USE.

Let us not walk to the utmost bounds of what we may, nor take so much liquor as perchance we may justify. It was permitted to the Jews to beat a malefactor with "forty stripes;" (Deut. xxv. 3;) yet they never exceeded nine-and-thirty, as appears by their scourging St. Paul, to whom, no doubt, they used their greatest cruelty. (2 Cor. xi. 24.) Let us not stretch our Christian liberty to the utmost. He that never will drink less than he may, sometimes will drink more than he should.

QUESTION.

But why is here mention of drunkenness only, and not of gluttony, seeing probably at such great feasts these twin vices go together?

ANSWER.

The apostle only instanceth in that sin which is most obvious, and appearing to sight. Gluttony is scarce discernible in him that is guilty of it. *Quia per esum necessitati voluptas miscetur, quid necessitas petat, et quid voluptas suppetat, ignoratur,* saith Gregory :* "Necessity in eating so incorporates itself with delight, that they are hardly to be distinguished." Besides, as thunder and lightning, though they come together, yet lightning first arriveth to our sight; so, though probably at the Corinthians' feasts gluttony and

---

* *Moral.*, lib. xxx., cap. 28, *ante medium.*

drunkenness were both joined together in the same person, yet drunkenness was soonest and easiest discerned.

VERSE 22.

What? have ye not houses to eat and drink in? or despise ye the church of God, and shame them that have not? What shall I say unto you? shall I praise you in this? I praise you not.

MUST you needs make the house of God the place of your feasting? If you be disposed to be merry, have ye not houses wherein ye may do it with more privacy and less offence? Or "despise you the church of God?" Do you undervalue the place set apart for God's service, to convert it into an ordinary banqueting-house? This is the exposition of all Greek writers, who expound it the material church; and their opinion is much favoured by the antithesis and opposition in the text, betwixt "church" and "houses." Hence it appears, that these love-feasts (which of late by the rich men's covetousness were enclosed into a private courtesy, which at the first were a common charity) were, to their greater abuse, kept in the church, or place of public meeting.

Only duties pious and public are to be performed in the church. Duties public and not pious more befit a guild-hall or town-house; duties pious and not public more become a closet: "Commune

with your heart in your chamber, and be still;"
(Psalm iv. 4;) whilst duties public and pious
beseem a church, as proper thereto.

USE.

To blame those that turn the church into a
counting-house, there to *rate* their neighbours,—
both to value their estates, and too often to revile
their persons. Others make it a market-place, there
to bargain in; yea, some turn it into a kennel
for their dogs, and a mew for their hawks, which
they bring with them. Surely if Christ drove out
thence sheep and doves, the emblems of inno-
cency, He would not have suffered these patterns of
cruelty to have abode in His temple.

But most Latin writers expound these words,
" Or despise ye the church of God?" of the spiritual church. The rich Corinthians, in not inviting
the poor, made balks* of good ground, chaff of
good corn; yea, refuse of God's elect.

OBJECTION.

But not inviting the poor, was not despising
them. A free-will offering is no debt. *In gratui-
tis nullā est injustitia.* Seeing therefore it had
been no sin in the Corinthians wholly to have
omitted their feasts, (as being not commanded by
God's word,) it could be no offence to exclude any
guest at their pleasure.

* [Ridges of land left unploughed, and therefore unproductive.—ED.]

ANSWER.

This is true of civil and ordinary entertainments: but these being entitled "love-feasts," and charity pretended the main motive of them, poor people were the most proper, should have been the most principal, guests. Besides, if not Christianity, yet civility,—if not grace, good nature,—might have moved them, whilst they gorged themselves, to have given something to the poor which stood by. To let them look on hungry, was a despising of them in a high degree, a *scandalum magnatum*, censurable in the Star-Chamber of Heaven; thus to wrong their peers in grace here, and glory hereafter.

DOCTRINE.

He that despiseth the poor, despiseth the church of God. Whereof they are a member inferior to none in piety; (God hath "chosen the poor of this world to be rich in faith," James ii. 5;) superior to all in number. Now he that pincheth the little toe paineth the whole body; the disgracing any member is the despising the whole church. Let us beware of affronting those in want, upbraiding their rags with our silks; setting our meat before their eyes, only to raise their appetites. "He that hath the things of this world, and seeth his brother to want, how doth the love of God dwell in him?"

And shame them that have not.

Not, that have not houses, though perchance but homely, and hired; but μὴ ἔχοντες, "those that have not" wealth and substance to pay the shot, and go to the cost to invite you again.

What shall I say? shall I praise you in this?

DOCTRINE.

Pastors may and must praise their people wherein they do well.

REASONS.

1. Hereby they shall peaceably possess themselves of the good-wills of their people, which may much advance the power and efficacy of their preaching. 2. Men will more willingly digest a reproof for their faults, if praised when they do well. 3. Virtue being commended doth increase and multiply; creepers in goodness will go, goers run, runners fly.

USE.

Those ministers to be blamed which are ever blaming, often without cause, always without measure; whereas it is said of God, "He will not be always chiding." (Psalm ciii. 9.) These preachers use their reproofs so commonly, till their physic turns natural, and will not work with their people.

Do any desire to hear that which Themistocles counted the best music,—namely, themselves commended? On these conditions, we ministers will indent with them: Let them find matter, we will find words; let them do what is commendable, and blame us if we commend not what they do. Such work for us would be recreation; such employment, a pleasure, turning our most stammering tongue into "the pen of a ready writer." To reprove is pressed from us, as wine from grapes; but praises would flow from our lips, as water from a fountain. But, alas! how can we build, when they afford us neither brick nor straw? How can we praise what they do, when they will not do what is to be praised? If with Ahab they will do what is evil, then with Micaiah we must always prophesy evil unto them.

In this I praise you not.

DOCTRINE.

Ministers must not commend their people when they do ill.

REASONS.

1. Dishonourable to God. 2. Dangerous to the ministers. That ambassador who, being sent to proclaim war, pronounceth peace to rebels, ("There is no peace, saith my God, to the wicked," Isai. lvii. 21,) deserves at his return to be preferred to the gallows. 3. Dangerous to the people, who are soothed in their sins. Honey-dews, though they

be sweet in taste, do black and blast the corn: so those who praise their people without cause, are cruelly kind unto them: it is pleasant to the palate of flesh, but destroyeth and damneth the soul.

USE.

It were to be wished, that as those that live under the equinoctial at noon-day, have no shadows at all; so great men should have no shadows, no parasites, no flatterers to commend them, when they least deserve it.

OBJECTION.

But why doth St. Paul deal so mildly with the Corinthians,—" I praise you not?" Methinks he should have made his little finger as heavy as his loins. " O ye Corinthians, I excommunicate every mother's child of you; I damn you all to the pit of hell, and deliver you to Satan, for your sin of drunkenness, at the receiving of the sacrament, never to be absolved but on your most serious and solemn repentance." Otherwise, considering the corrupt humour in the Corinthians, the apostle's purge was too gentle for them.

ANSWER.

1. Theophylact answers, that St. Paul reproves the rich men the more mildly, lest otherwise they should be implacably incensed against the poor, fretting against them, as the causers of the apostle's anger.

2. It was the first time he told the Corinthians

of their fault; and therefore used them the more gently, on hope of their amendment. This corrupt humour in the Corinthians was not as yet grown tough, baked and clodded in them by custom, and therefore the easier purged and removed.

OBSERVATION.

Ministers must use mildness, especially at their first reproving of a sin. Yea, God so blessed the mild severity of St. Paul, that the Corinthians reformed all their errors; for no fault reprehended by the apostle in them in this first Epistle, is taxed again in the second Epistle; a very strong presumption that all those faults were amended.

Now, whereas we find such abuses in the church of Corinth, presently after it was newly planted; we may learn

DOCTRINE.

Corruptions will quickly creep into the best church. Thus St. Paul no sooner went back from the Galatians, but they went back from his doctrine. Gal. v. 7: " Ye did run well; who did hinder you?" And as we read of Mezentius, a cruel tyrant, who joined dead corpses to living men, and so killed them with lingering torments; so some seducers in the church of Galatia sought to couple the lively grace of God and active faith with the dead letter of the law, and old legal ceremonies long since dead, buried, and rotten, in the grave of our Saviour.

USE.

"If it be done thus to the green tree, what shall be done to the dry?" If primitive churches, whilst the apostles which planted them were alive to prune them, had such errors in them, no wonder if the church at sixteen hundred years of age may have some defaults. Moses said unto the Israelites, "Behold, while I am alive with you this day, ye have been rebellious against the Lord; and how much more when I am dead?" (Deut. xxxi. 27.) So if, while St. Paul survived, churches were so prone to decline, what can be less expected in our days? It was therefore well concluded in the thirty-ninth session of the Council of Constance,* that every ten years, at the farthest, there should be a General Council held, to reform such errors in the church as probably in that time would arise.

VERSE 23.

For I have received of the Lord that which I also delivered unto you, That the Lord Jesus the same night in which He was betrayed took bread.

AFTER he had fully reproved the corruptions of their love-feasts, cometh he now to reduce the receiving of the sacrament to the first institution of Christ.

* Fox, Martyrol., p. 594.

OBSERVATION.

It is the safest way to correct all the Errata's in the transcript according to the original copy. Thus did Christ in the matter of divorce: "But from the beginning it was not so." (Matt. xix. 8.) Excellently St. Cyprian: "We must not heed what others did, who were before us; but what Christ did, who was before all."

USE.

Were this used betwixt us and the Papists, to clear the stream of God's service by the fountain of its first institution, how soon would seven sacraments shrink to two! how quickly would cream, oil, and spittle fly out of baptism, and leave nothing but fair water behind! How soon, &c.

For I have received of the Lord.

QUESTION.

How could St. Paul receive it of the Lord, with whom he never conversed in the flesh, being "one born out of time," as he confesseth of himself?

ANSWER.

He received it, 1. Mediately, by Ananias, who began with him where Gamaliel ended. 2. Besides, (lest the Corinthians should say that they received it likewise at the second hand, as well as St. Paul,) he had it immediately from God. Gal. i. 12: "For I neither received it of man, neither was I taught it, but by the revelation of Jesus Christ."

I also delivered unto you.

The Greek is, παρέδωκα ὑμῖν. Latin, *Tradidi vobis.* English it as you please, " I traditioned it unto you." *Nota,* saith A Lapide on this place, *hunc locum pro traditionibus quas orthodoxi verbo Dei scripto adjungendas docent.* Bellarmine also starts traditions out of the same place. What eye-salve are their eyes anointed with, that can see unwritten traditions here, when the apostle delivereth nothing but is recorded in three evangelists, Matthew, Mark, Luke?

However, hence we will take occasion briefly to speak of unwritten traditions; the church of Rome maintaining that the Scriptures of themselves are too scant to salvation, except the course list of unwritten traditions be cast in to make measure; and this they will have of equal authority with the written word.

FOUR OBSERVATIONS CONCERNING TRADITIONS.

Mark by the way, 1. This is the reason why Romanists are so zealous for traditions; for, finding themselves cast by the Scriptures, they would fain appeal to another judge: yea, hereon are founded those points which get them their gain, as purgatory, and the appurtenances thereof. Hath not Demetrius, then, reason to stand for

Diana, (Acts xix. 25,) when his goods and her godship must go together?

2. Though they lock up the Scriptures in an unknown language, and forbid the laity to read them, yet they suffer traditions to be preached and published to all in general. Such wooden daggers will never hurt Popery to the heart; and therefore they suffer their children to play with these dull tools, though not to handle the " two-edged sword " of God's Word.

3. Romanists will never give us a perfect list and catalogue of their traditions, that we may know their set number, how many there be of them; but still reckon them up with an *et cætera*, leave still a *plus ultra* to place more in if need require. And as the Athenians, for fear they should omit any deity, erected an altar " to the unknown God;" so the Papists, in summing up their traditions, will not complete their number, but are careful to leave blanks and void places for a refuge and retreating place, that, in case they be pressed in disputation, and cannot prove their point by places of Scripture, they may still plead it is a " tradition."

4. Whereas the word " tradition " is taken in several senses, and there be many kinds of them, Papists jumble and confound them together. As cheaters use to cast their counterfeit coin amongst good gold, hoping so to pass it away current and

undiscovered; so they shuffle false and true traditions together in one heap, that the bad may go off under the countenance and protection of the good. We will mar their mart, by sorting them into these several ranks:

(1.) "Traditions" in a general sense are taken for things delivered, though in Scripture, by Christ and His apostles. Thus St. Basil* calls baptizing "in the name of the F[ather], S[on], and H[oly] G[host]," a "tradition.

(2.) For such matters of faith which are not found in Scripture *totidem verbis*, in the words and sound, but yet in the same sense and substance, or at least may by faithful consequence be thence deduced; as the Trinity of persons; two wills in Christ; His consubstantiality with God the Father. Thus Lindan, a Papist, calls original sin a "tradition."

(3.) For such opinions against which nothing appears in Scripture, and the church in all times and ages has maintained them, condemning the opposers for erroneous; as that the mother of Christ was ever a virgin.

(4.) For such rites and ceremonies of the church (no matters of faith) which therein have been used from great antiquity; and therefore probably might have their original from the apostles; as fasting in Lent, though the manner, time, and

* *Contra Eunomium*, lib. iii.

continuance in keeping it was very different in several churches.

Take "traditions" in the first and second acception, we account them to have equal force and authority with the written word. In the third sense we honour and embrace them as true. In the last acception we approve and practise them as decent and ancient; provided always they be not obtruded as things necessary to salvation, but indifferent in their nature.

But all this makes nothing for the black guard of Romish traditions, which lag still behind:— some of them frivolous; as this " apostolical tradition," * that a priest, if against their wills they receive any money from wicked men, they must in no case expend it on meat, but to buy wood and coals. Some impious and blasphemous; worshipping of images, prayers to saints, the sacrifice of the mass, purgatory, &c., having nothing for them, much against them, in God's written word.

To draw to a conclusion: Scriptures, besides many others, have two most principal privileges above traditions.

1. First, their infallibility, as being inspired by the Spirit of God. 2 Pet. i. 20 : "So that ye first know this, that no prophecy of the Scripture is of any private interpretation." Verse 21 : "For the prophecy came not in old time

* Clemens Rom., lib. xl., cap. 10, *Apost. Constit*

by the will of man: but holy men of God spake as they were moved by the Holy Ghost." As for the authors of traditions, they might both *falli* and *fallere*, "be deceived" themselves, and "deceive" others. They might be deceived themselves, either by misunderstanding the traditions delivered unto them, or by misremembering, or by misrelating them again. They might deceive others, either unwillingly by these forenamed slips and infirmities, or else willingly and wittingly by venting those things as received from the apostles which they had not received from them, and by usurpation entitling the fancies of their own heads to be apostolical precepts.

2. The Providence of God plainly appears in His preserving of the Scriptures against all oppositions. "Many a time from my youth up," may the Scriptures now say, "yea, many a time have they fought against me from my youth; but they could not prevail against me." Neither Antiochus before Christ, nor Julian the Apostate since him, nor the force of tyrants, nor the fraud of heretics, (though the world of late hath scarce yielded a wicked sharp wit that hath not given the Scriptures a gash,) could ever suppress them. Their treading on this camomile made it grow the better; and their snuffing of this candle made it burn the brighter. Whereas, on the other side, the records of *traditions* are lost; and those books wherein they

were compiled and composed, *aut incuriâ hominum, aut injuriâ temporis*, or by some other sinister accident, are wholly miscarried, and nowhere appear. Papias is reported by Eusebius* in five books to have contained all the apostolical traditions, which they call " the word not written,"—by Bellarmine himself confessed, that these are lost. Likewise Clemens Alexandrinus, as the same Eusebius storieth it,† wrote in a book those traditions which he received from the elders, and they from the apostles; which book the Papists themselves at this day cannot produce.

I will conclude all with Gamaliel's words, Acts v. 39 : " But if it be of God, ye cannot destroy it." Had these books been inspired by God's Spirit, no doubt the same Providence would have watched to preserve them which hath protected the Scripture. Let us, therefore, leaving uncertain traditions, stick to the Scriptures alone; trust no doctrine on its single bond, which brings not God's word for its security. Let that plate be beaten in pieces, which hath not this "Tower-stamp" upon it.

That the Lord Jesus the same night wherein He was betrayed.

OBSERVATION.

Christ bestowed the greatest courtesy on mankind, when He foresaw that He should receive the greatest

* *Hist.*, lib. iv., cap. 8. † *Hist.*, lib. vi., cap. 11.

cruelty from them. O that we were like-minded with our Saviour, to move fastest in piety when we draw nearest the centre of death, and then chiefly to study to fasten favours on our enemies!

QUESTION.

Why did Christ institute it then, and not before?

ANSWER.

1. Because dying men bequeath not their legacies till they make their wills, nor departing friends bestow their tokens till they take their farewell.

2. Because, till then, the passover (a sacrament in the same kind) did continue in full force; and the Lord's Supper was not to be lighted, till the Passover was first fairly put out.

QUESTION.

Seeing Christ appointed it a supper, how comes it now to be a dinner?

ANSWER.

God hath intrusted the discretion of His church, on just occasion, to alter some circumstances in the sacrament. True it is, such circumstances as are sacramental, not only of the *commission at large*, but also of the *Quorum nomina*, whose absence or alteration maims and mangles the sacrament, are unchangeable. But common and ordinary circumstances (such as is the time, place, kind of bread and wine) the church hath power to alter, by virtue of a warrant left to it by Christ; " Let all things be done decently, and in order."

REASONS OF THE CHANGE.

It was turned into a dinner, 1. To avoid the inconveniences which a full stomach surfeited and surcharged will bring, as in the Corinthians.

2. That our bodies, which are like new barrels, whiles we are fasting, may first be seasoned with the liquor of Christ's blood.

Let us thank God that we are not necessitated to receive the communion in the night, as in the primitive church, in time of persecution, when Christians, to drink Christ's blood, did adventure the losing of their own.

Took bread.

QUESTION.

Why did Christ choose so cheap and common a thing to exhibit His body in?

ANSWER.

1. Herein He graciously provided for the poor. Had He appointed some rich and costly recipe, the estate of the poor could not procure it for themselves, and the charity of the rich would not purchase it for others.

2. Had He instituted it in some dear and precious element, happily people would have imputed the efficacy thereof to its natural worth and work-

ing, not to Christ's institution. Christ therefore chooseth plain bread; a thing so mean in itself, it is not within suspicion to eclipse God of His glory; none can be so mad as to attribute to plain bread itself such spiritual operation.

Let us take heed how we take snuff at the simplicity of God's ordinance. Say not with Naaman, "Is not Abana and Pharpar," &c. Is not the bread in the baker's panniers, and the wine in the vintner's cellar, as good as that which is propounded in the sacrament? And far be it from us to seek with our own inventions to beguard that which God will have plain. Rather let us pray, that our eyes may be anointed with that eye-salve, to see majesty in the meanness, and the state in the simplicity, of the sacraments.

QUESTION.

But amongst such variety of others, such cheap elements to represent Christ's body in, why was bread preferred above all?

ANSWER.

To show our bodies can as well subsist without bread, as our souls without a Saviour. It is called " the staff of bread;" other meats are but as pretty wands to whisk in our hands. Without bread no feast; with bread no famine.

VERSE 24.

And when He had given thanks, He brake it, and said, Take, eat: this is My body, which is broken for you: this do in remembrance of Me.

And when He had given thanks, εὐχαριστήσας.

So it is Luke xxvi. 19: but St. Matthew, chap. xxvi. 26, hath it εὐλογήσας, "He blessed." Yet let not these two words fall out; for they are brethren, of affinity in sense and signification. At this day εὐχαριστήσας, "He gived thanks," hath christened the whole service of the eucharist.

DOCTRINE.

Whensoever we are to receive any food, we are to give God thanks, but especially at the sacrament.

REASONS.

1. It is our duty. God, the Lord paramount of the world, though He hath made us in Christ freeholders of all His creatures, yet hath reserved thanks as a quick rent for Himself.

2. It is profitable for us. 1 Tim. iv. 4, 5: "For every creature of God is good, and nothing to be refused, if it be received with thanksgiving; for it is sanctified by the word of God and prayer." Yea, thanksgiving makes every creature both chew the cud, and cleave the hoof. The physician may forbid one meat, the divine cannot; it may be against one's health, not one's conscience. Tue,

the Jews' life was a constant Lent, from much forbidden meat; but Christians, paying thanks to God, buy a licence to eat anything.

He brake it.

To signify how His body should be broken for mankind. Whilst therefore the priest in the sacrament breaketh the bread, let the people's meditation attend his action, and conceive they see Christ's head, back, hands, feet, side, broken with the thorns, whips, nails, spear. And hence it appeareth, that the celebrating of Christ's body in broken bread, is more natural to Christ's institution, and more expressive in itself, than, as the church of Rome doth, in a whole and entire wafer.

And said unto them, Take.

That is, take it in their hands, and put it to their mouth; not as the custom lately induced in the Romish church, for the priest to put it in the mouth of every communicant.

OBJECTION.

But it is pleaded for the Popish custom, that it is unmannerly for laymen to handle Christ's body; and therefore it is most reverence to take it with their mouths.

ANSWER.

1. There is no such clown in Christianity as he

who will be more mannerly than God will have him. It is most reverence for us to do as God commands us. Ahaz tempted God in saying, he "would not tempt Him," when God bid him "ask a sign." (Isai. vii. 12.) Those do little better, who, more nice than wise, strain courtesy not to take Christ's body in their hands, when He reaches it.

2. Take it strictly, and our mouths are as unworthy as our hands to receive Christ's body. No more sanctity in the one than in the other, being both made of the same lump of flesh. But, seeing it is Christ's pleasure to come under the roof of our mouth, let Him also pass through the porch of our hands. The rather because it seemeth that we entertain Christ's body in more state, and with more observance towards it, when the more servants attend it, the more members of our body using their service in receiving it.

3. Lastly, the Romish custom in putting it into their mouths loseth the expression and significancy of the hand of faith. The taking Christ's body in our hands mindeth us spiritually by faith to apprehend and lay hold on His mercies and merits.

T. C.[*] NEEDLESS CAVIL.

And here let us take notice of the needless

[*] [Probably Thomas Cartwright, the great Puritan divine, who was the leader of the Nonconformists during Queen Elizabeth's reign.—ED.]

cavil of such as snarl at the practice of our English church, because, whereas Christ said in a generality, once for all, to His disciples, "Take and eat," our church speaketh it to every particular person. We answer, This is no considerable variation from Christ's form; for, first, it appears not in the text to the contrary but that Christ might speak these words severally to each apostle, though it be not expressed, because histories truss up things in bundles, and, omitting particulars, set down only the total sum. Secondly, God hath intrusted the ministers of His church to spin out His universal precepts and promises into particulars. Thus, Matt. xxviii. 19, Christ saith, "Teach all nations, baptizing them in the name of the Father," &c.: which the priest, by the consent of all churches, applieth to each infant: "I baptize thee," &c.

This is My body.

That is, that which signifies, signs, and presents My body, and sacramentally is My body, and which, received with faith, seals to thee all the benefits of My death and passion, not transubstantiated into My body, according to the Popish opinion, whereof briefly.

The doctrine of transubstantiation was first occasioned by the unwary speeches of Damascene and Theophylact. These, seeing no present, and foreseeing no future, errors about the sacraments, were too transcendent and hyperbolical in their expressions about the real presence of Christ in the sacrament. Thus, as oftentimes *lascivia calami*, the dashes and flourishes of a scrivener over-active with his pen, have afterwards been mistaken to be letters really intended; so the witty extravagancies and rhetorical phrases of these fathers were afterward interpreted to be their distilled doctrinal positions: so dangerous it is for any to wanton it with their wits in mysteries of religion. But transubstantiation was never made an article of faith, till the Council of Lateran; no penalty imposed on the maintainers of the contrary, till the Council of Trent. But let us hear some of their arguments.

ARGUMENT I.

The text saith, "This is My body;" and therefore it is so plainly to be understood. For Scripture admits of a figurative sense as its refuge, not as its choice; only *se defendere,* "to shield and shelter itself" from nonsense and contradictions: otherwise the literal sense is to be embraced. And therefore the Holy Spirit is so here to be understood, "This is truly My body."

ANSWER.

From the literal understanding of these words

flow many absurdities; and therefore we are forced to fly to a figurative meaning. Philosophy brings in an army of impossibilities; as, that the same body at the same time should be in several places; that accidents should subsist without a substance, &c. To wave these, the antiquity of faith excepts against it, it destroys the nature of a sacrament; the same thing cannot be the sign and seal of Christ's body, and the very body in substance.

ARGUMENT II.

We are not to measure God's arm by our eye, His power by our understanding; wherefore, *non obstante* all pretended impossibility, God doth turn the bread into His Son's body; for nothing is impossible unto Him.

ANSWER.

Were it expressed in Scripture, that it were God's will to turn the bread into Christ's flesh, we would work ourselves to believe it, and make reason strike sail to faith. So it is not God's power we question, but His will and pleasure.

ARGUMENT III.

But He saith, *totidem verbis*, "This is My body;" and dying men use to speak most plainly; with them figures are out of date, the flowers of rhetoric fade; especially they write without welt or guard in their wills and testaments.

ANSWER.

A familiar trope or figure is as plain as no figure. Even a child in age is man enough to understand, " Cool the pot," " Drink off that cup." Yea, many speak figures,. who know not what figures mean. Besides, Christ at His death spake no other language than what His tongue and His disciples' ears were used to in His lifetime: " I am the Vine; I am the Way; I am the Door." He who is so sottish as to conceive that Christ was a material door, showeth himself to be a *post* indeed.

Which is broken for you.

The flesh of Christ was afterwards on the cross literally broken; there was *solutio continui*, with the nails in His hands and feet. As for His bones, (John xix. 36,) " not a bone of Him " was " broken " in the literal sense. But virtually and eminently, in the same meaning wherein it is said " a broken heart," all his bones were broken, that is, contrited and grinded with grief and sorrow.

Do this.

In Latin, *Hoc facite*, which the Papists expound sacrifice; this according to Virgil's verse,

" *Cùm faciam vitulâ pro frugibus, ipse venito.*" *

So much is the church of Rome beholden to this poet, both for the sacrifice of the mass out of his Eclogues, and *limbus patrum* out of the first book

* [Ecl. iii., 77.—ED.]

of his Æneads. But seeing this action, "Do this," is enjoined as well to the people as the priest; and seeing none but the priest could offer *proprii nominis sacrificium;* it plainly appears this cannot here be a proper sacrifice.

In remembrance.

DOCTRINE.

Wherein this doctrine is intimated: *Men are prone to forget God's favours unto them, except they be minded of them.* The Israelites had not this great goodness in remembrance; but were disobedient "at the sea, even at the Red Sea." (Psalm cvi. 7.) Who would have thought that the deliverance at the Red Sea would so soon have been drowned in a deeper Sea of Oblivion?

REASONS OF OUR FORGETFULNESS.

1. The devil's malice; who, whilst we sleep in idleness and negligence, stealeth into the memory, the Muniment House of the soul, and embezzleth and purloineth from thence the records of most moment and importance.

2. But not to play the devil with the devil, not to accuse him falsely, he is not the principal cause of our forgetfulness, which floweth chiefly from the corruption of our nature; which, like a bolter, lets all the flour pass, and keeps only the bean behind.

But here we must not understand the bare naked and empty remembrance of Christ's death, the calling to mind the history of His passion; (which the devils can do, and the worst of men;) thus to remember Christ were but to forget Him;—but a remembrance *cum effectu*, the relying on His death with a lively faith, and applying His merits to our souls. Whereof more largely hereafter.

Of Me

Incarnated, "of Me" born, "of Me" circumcised, "of Me" baptized, "of Me" tempted, "of Me" scourged, but especially "of Me" crucified, and also "of Me" ascended, and now glorified.

VERSE 25.

After the same manner also He took the cup, when He had supped, saying, This cup is the New Testament in My blood; this do ye, as oft as ye drink it, in remembrance of Me.

FOLLOWETH now the other part of the sacrament instituted in the wine. He doubleth the elements, to show that in Christ is not only necessary and sufficient, but also plentiful and abundant, with assured, redemption.

To blame then [is] the church of Rome, whose Levites are guilty of that fault whereof Benjamin was taxed; they have "stolen away the cup." If "to steal the chalice" be the phrase whereby men express the highest sin, what sacrilege is it to steal the *wine* of the chalice, from whom it belongeth? But it is a wonder if old thieves be taken without an excuse; let us hear what these Romanists plead for themselves.

OBJECTION I.

Nature hath so put flesh and blood in a joint patent, that they go always together. Where there is one, there are both; and where not both, neither. It is superfluous therefore to give the laity the blood the second time, who by concomitancy had received it before.

ANSWER I.

Indeed, flesh and blood, like loving playmates, were together in Christ's body, till torments forced them to part asunder. Now we are to receive Christ's blood "shed," not as it was at home, housed in heaviness; but as pain banished it abroad and poured it out. Wherefore, what God hath put asunder, to be taken severally and distinctly, let no man join together.

OBJECTION II.

But there be many inconveniences, yea, mischiefs, attend the laity's receiving of the wine; as, its sticking in their beards, spilling of it, &c.

ANSWER II.

Non debemus esse sapientiores legibus. God, in

the omnisciency of His wisdom, surveyed the latitude of all occurrences, yet, beholding all future inconveniences present, He appointed the laity to drink of the cup. Wine was then as subject to spilling; it hath not since gotten a more liquid or diffusive quality.

OBJECTION III.

But in several places of Scripture no mention is made of wine, but of bread only; as Acts ii. 42, and 46, "continued breaking of bread from house to house;" Acts xx. 7, "met together to break bread."

ANSWER III.

Either "bread," by a synecdoche, is here put for bread and wine; or else that phrase importeth their ordinary meetings and civil feasts. But a cart-load of these exceptions, *Tekel*, are "weighed in the balance, and found too light" to outpoise Christ's institution. The wise Shunammite woman (2 Kings iv. 30) was not content with the company of Elisha's staff and servant; but, "As the Lord liveth," saith she, "and as thy soul liveth, I will not leave thee;" she would not lean on the staff, but on the staff's master, and would have him with her. So let us not be so foolish [as] to depart from God's written word in the sacrament, concerning giving the laity the cup, for the company of human arguments on our side; but let us stick close to our commission, and then we need not fear a *Præmunire,* so long as we have the letter of God's law on our side.

When He had supped.

Christ did therefore institute this sacrament after supper, to show that herein He chiefly aimed not at the feeding of our bodies, but the refreshing of our souls. We are not to bring our devotion in our guts, and to come to the communion for belly cheer; like those that followed our Saviour, (John vi. 26,) because they had "eaten of the loaves, and were filled." No, we are to come with more refined thoughts, and, as for matter of bodily meat, contain ourselves as after supper.

This cup is the new testament in My blood.

"This cup," that is, the wine in this cup. We cannot scarce stir a pace in Scripture without meeting with a figure, even in these testamentary expressions of our Saviour. Why, then, do the Papists make such news, yea, wonders, at figures, than which nothing is more common? "Is the new testament in My blood;" that is, the wine therein contained signeth unto you the new covenant of grace, which is ratified and confirmed in My blood; that is, by My death. For indeed it is the death of the testator that giveth life to the testament; and the will, though sealed, is not sealed in effect, till the maker of the same be dead.

But why is it called "the new testament," seeing it is an old one, and the same which was made to Adam, ("The Seed of the woman shall break the serpent's head,") often reiterated and confirmed to Abraham, David, and others?

Indeed, it was old in the promise, new in the performance; old *quoad substantiam et materiam fœderis,* new *quoad modum clarioris manifestationis.* It is said of those that live within a mile or two of Olympus, that they are under a constant and continued shade, which the height of the mountain casteth upon them. So the Jews, and all the church of God before Christ's coming, lived in constant umbrages and shadows of types, figures, ceremonies, and representations; all which were taken away, when our Saviour, "the Sun of Righteousness," did appear. Therefore it is said, "in My blood," as in opposition to the blood of kids, calves, goats sacrificed in the temple. Other parts of the verse are expounded in the former.

VERSE 26.

For as often as ye eat of this bread, and drink this cup, ye do show the Lord's body * *till He come.*

UNDER "as often" is "often" included; whence

* ["The Lord's *death*" is the rendering of our present Authorized Version, and accords with the original,—τὸν θάνατον τοῦ Κυρίου. —ED.]

we gather, *we must frequently celebrate the Lord's Supper.* In the primitive church it was done every day: * and fit it was the *aqua vitæ* bottle should ever be at their nostrils, who were sounding every moment; and they needed constant cordials, who ever and anon had the qualms of temptation in the time of persecution. This frequency soon abated, when peace came into the church; which makes St. Ambrose † reprove the negligence of the eastern churches, who received it but once a year. At this day our mother church of England, seeing her children's backwardness herein, by canon compelleth them to receive at the least thrice a year: such is the necessity to force them by law to come to a feast, and to make a statute for hungry men to eat, and sick folk to take physic. But hear the arguments of some to the contrary, that it is to be but seldom received.

OBJECTION I.

The passover was celebrated but once a year; in whose place (for sacraments never die without heirs) the Lord's Supper succeeds.

ANSWER I.

The passover by God was stinted to be used no oftener; in the Lord's Supper we are left to our

* Eusebius, *Demonst. Evang.*, lib. i., cap. 10.
† *De Sacramentis*, lib. v., cap. 4.

own liberty. Finding therefore our continual sinning, and therefore need thereof to strengthen us in our grace, we may, yea, must oftener use it, especially seeing all services of God under the Gospel ought to be more plentiful and abundant than under the law.

OBJECTION II.

Things done often are seldom done solemnly. Manna, if rained every day, is not dainty. The frequent doing of it will make men perfunctory and negligent therein.

ANSWER II.

Necessary duties are not to be left undone for the inconveniences which, *per accidens*, through human corruption may follow thereon. Then sermons should be as seldom as Apollo's smiles, *semel in anno;* and prayers should not be presented to God every day, lest the commonness of the duty should bring it into contempt. Rather ministers are to instruct their people to come with reverence, notwithstanding their frequent repairing thereunto.

OBJECTION III.

But long preparation is requisite to this action; and therefore this sacrament cannot often be received.

ANSWER III.

After the first grand preparation, whereby faith and repentance we are first estated in God's favour, other preparations are not so difficult in doing, or tedious in time, as being but the reiterating of the same again. The good housewife that scoureth her plate once a week, hath less work than she that doth it but once in [a] twelvemonth. Often preparing makes the work easy, and fits men the sooner for the sacrament: though I am not altogether of St. Ambrose's opinion,* that *qui non meretur quotidie accipere, non meretur post annum accipere.*

QUESTION.

Whether is it of absolute necessity, that a man on his deathbed should receive the sacrament?

ANSWER.

He is as weak in judgment as the dying man in body, who conceives it so. It is not the bare absence, but the neglect and contempt of the sacrament, which is dangerous. Besides, that surely is not by God made absolutely necessary to salvation, which in some cases is impossible to be had: as in sudden death, when the sick man is gone before the priest can come; in infectious diseases, when the priest cannot bring Christ's blood without the hazarding of his own; not to speak of the inconveniency of giving it to those who go out of the world for pain to bring others into it.

Yea, of such persons, who desire the sacrament,

* *Loco priùs citato.*

I find three sorts. Some do it out of mere fancy, who desire it because they desire it; (like David's longing for the water of the well of Bethlehem;) can give no account of their humour therein. A second sort, out of superstition. A third, out of a true faith, and feeling of their infirmity. Now charity "thinketh no ill; hopeth all things." We ministers believe all to be of the later sort, and will not think much of our pains to tender our service unto them, when sent for: but be it betwixt God and their consciences; let them take heed how they abuse God's ambassadors, and cause us to come on foolish occasions, to feed their own fancies.

*You do show forth the Lord's body.**

DOCTRINE.

The sacrament, solemnly celebrated, doth represent and set forth the passion of Christ. This is the meaning of St. Paul, Galat. iii. 1: "O foolish Galatians, who hath bewitched you, that you should not obey the truth, before whose eyes Jesus Christ hath been evidently set forth, crucified among you?" That is, Christ was so powerfully and pathetically preached unto them in the word, His death so done to the life in the solemn, decent, and expressive administration of the sacrament, that the tragedy of Christ's death nigh Jerusalem was re-acted before them.

* [See note on p. 64.—ED.]

USE.

Say not then in thine heart, "How shall I get to Jerusalem, to see the place of Christ's suffering?" See, faith can remove mountains; Mount Calvary is brought home to thee; and though there be μέγα χάσμα, "a great gulf," or distance of ground, betwixt England and Palestine, yet, if thou beest a faithful receiver, behold Christ sacramentally crucified on the communion table. Say not in thine heart, "How shall I remember Christ's passion? It was 'time out of mind,' sixteen hundred years ago." Christ here teacheth thee the art of memory; what so long was past is now made present at the instant of thy worthy receiving. Stay, pilgrims, stay! (would your voyages to the Holy Land had been as far from superstition as hitherto from success!) go not you thither, but bring Palestine hither, by bringing pure hearts with you, when you come to receive the sacrament; for there the Lord's body is "showed forth," as on the cross.

Till He come.

OBSERVATION.

God, till the world's end, when He cometh to judgment, will have a church on earth, wherein pastors shall administer, and people receive, the sacrament.

Witness His promise before His death, Matt.

xvi. 18: "And the gates of hell shall not prevail against it;" and another after His resurrection, Matt. xxviii. 20: "And, lo, I am with you alway unto the end of the world;" with you in yourselves and successors, persons and posterity. Indeed, the church may want things of lustre, never of essence: it may want a glorious being, never a being: *Deus non deerit in necessariis.* The church is like the sun, which may be clouded and eclipsed, yet still remaineth "a faithful witness." (Psalm lxxxix. 37.) Besides, churches may fall away, but the *church* cannot; the setting of the Gospel in one place will be the rising of it in another. This is meant Rev. ii. 5: "I will remove thy candlestick out of his place;" not, "I will quench or put out thy candle," but, "I will remove it," so that it shall still remain in one place or other, "till I come." And then sacraments shall be celebrated no more, but types shall give place to the truth, and shadows shall yield to the substance. Then all the week shall be one constant Sabbath, and yet therein no sermons preached, nor prayers made, but all our liturgy shall be praising of God. And now what remaineth, but that we cry from our hearts with the saints? "Come, Lord Jesus; come quickly.'"

VERSE 27.

Wherefore whosoever shall eat this bread, and drink this cup of the Lord, unworthily, shall be guilty of the body and blood of the Lord.

Lo, these two words present us with two principal parts: 1. The sin. 2. The sinfulness of the sin.

The sin is the unworthy eating and drinking of the bread and wine of the Lord.

QUESTION.

Is any man so well stored with grace, that he can eat these sacraments worthily?

ANSWER.

One may do an action worthily in a threefold respect.

THREEFOLD WORTHINESS.

1. First, worthily *dignitate æqualitatis*, as "the labourer is worthy of his hire." (Luke x. 7.) This exact worthiness may claim and challenge a reward due unto it, and the denier or detainer doth this worthy party wrong and injury. Now no saint can receive with this God's-justice-proof worthiness, as appears by their humble confessions, not out of compliment, but consciousness of their faults: Jacob, Gen. xxxii. 10: John Baptist, Matt. iii. 11. Yea, this worthiness is waved by our church liturgy, at the Communion,

both (as I may say) in our grace before meat,— "We be not worthy so much as to gather up the crumbs under Thy table;" and in our grace after meat,—"And though we be unworthy through our manifold sins to offer unto Thee," &c.

2. The second is, worthily *dignitate convenientiæ, aptitudinis,* or *decentiæ;* which consists, though not in a perfect and exact proportion, yet in some fitness, meetness, and likeness unto that which is required. Such phrases are frequent in Scripture. Matt. iii. 8 : "Bring forth therefore fruits worthy of repentance;" that is, such as bear no open repugnancy and contradiction to the repentance you profess, but in some sort meet and agreeing thereunto. So, "walk worthy of the Lord;" (Col. i. 10;) "worthy your calling;" (Eph. iv. 1;) "worthy the Gospel." (Phil. i. 27.) That is, let not your life shame your belief; break not the Commandments against the Creed; let not your practice be ἀσύστατος ["inconsistent"] with your profession. And we must know, that *peccata surreptitia,* sins of infirmity, (not through their want of wickedness, but God's store of mercy,) may stand and subsist with this worthiness of conveniency. In this acception we understand in my text to "eat worthily;" that is, so fitted and prepared as may bear some resemblance and agreement to the solemnity of the work we go about.

3. There remaineth a third kind of worthiness, which is *dignitas dignationis;* the worthiness of acceptance, when God for Christ's sake is pleased to take our actions in good worth. That is well spoken which is well taken; and that man is worthy who by God is accepted so to be. Indeed, if base and ignorant people should cry one up to be worthy, and prize pebbles to be pearls, he is no whit the better for the over-valuing of him; but if God pleaseth to esteem men worthy, things are as they are accounted by Him; His valuing of them puts worth into them. "I have blessed him," saith Isaac of Jacob; (Gen. xxvii. 33;) "yea, and he shall be blessed." God hath accounted them worthy; yea, and they shall be worthy; as it is Rev. iii. 4: "They shall walk with Me in white: for they are worthy." Let us, when we come to the sacrament, bring with us the worthiness of fitness and convenience; and God of His goodness will be pleased to reward us with the worthiness of acceptance.

Two sorts of people, then, do eat and drink unworthily. First, the *unregenerate*, those which, as it is Heb. vi. 1, have not as yet "laid the foundation of repentance from dead works, and faith" in Christ, but remain still in their pure, impure naturals, not ingrafted into Christ. Without this foundation, the fair side-walls of a good nature, and the proud roof of all moral performances, will both totter and tumble to the ground. Secondly, the *regenerate*, but guilty of some sins unrepented of, who eat unworthily till they have sued out a special pardon out of the Court of Heaven.

Come we now to the sinfulness of the sin. "Shall be guilty of the body and blood of the Lord;" that is, they are offenders in the same form with Judas and the Jews, guilty of shedding the blood and wounding the body of Christ. For, as those that deface the stamp or abuse the seal of a king, are entituled to be traitors; so the unworthy receivers of these elements, which personate and represent Christ's body, are interpreted to sin against the body of Christ itself. Some Protestants have, by God's providence, escaped in their persons; and yet the Papists, to manifest their spite, have burned their pictures at a stake. Christ's person is shot-free from any man's malice, out of the reach of your cruelty, sitting at the right hand of God in heaven: as for His picture, it is with us in the sacraments; and unworthy receivers show to the shadow what they would do to the substance, if it were in their power; they push as far as their short horns will give them leave.

OBJECTION.

But, may one say, grant unworthy receiving be a grievous sin, yet methinks too heavy an accent is put upon it to equalize it with the murdering of Christ. Jonathan said, "I did but taste a little honey with the end of my rod, and, lo, I must die;" (1 Sam. xiv. 43;) but more justly and grievously may the wicked communicant complain, "I did but eat a morsel of bread, and drank a draught of wine, and, lo, I must die here, hereafter, temporally and eternally; yea, my sin is heightened to be even with the sin of Judas and the Jews, who wilfully imbrued their hands in Christ's blood."

ANSWER.

However human corruption may be the advocate to plead herein, yet we must count sins to be so great as God esteems them to be. He "seeth not as man seeth," nor judgeth He as man judgeth. He will judge that to be pride, which we count to be good carriage; that lust, which we count love; that drunkenness, which we good fellowship; and unworthy receiving, which we perchance esteem a fault, but not of the first magnitude, He judgeth it the highest of any pardonable sin, even guiltiness of Christ's blood itself. Learn we from hence to measure and survey a sin in the true height, length, and breadth thereof. Hearken not to the partiality of thine own flesh, which will make thine offences in number less, in nature lighter. Listen not to the suggestions of Satan, which will never suffer us to see our sins truly, but is always in the excess or defect. When we go on in a sinful course, he bears us in hand that our sins are small; and when we are touched in conscience, he seeks to persuade us that they are too great, mountains too big to be drowned in the ocean of God's mercy. But let us measure them by the square of God's word, an infallible rule that will not deceive us.

To conclude: men generally hate Pilate and Judas: if we see them but in pictures, our blood riseth at them, we could scratch them out with our nails; being more angry with them than David with the rich man that took away the poor man's ewe lamb; whereas in some sense it may be said of many of us, "Thou art the man." Yet, as for those which hitherto have not taken notice of the heinousness of this sin, and through the want of consideration have been "guilty of the body of" Christ; let me say to them what St. Peter doth, Acts iii. 17: "And now, brethren, I wot that through ignorance you did it. Repent therefore, and be converted, that your sins may be blotted out." And let us all pray with David, Psalm li. 14: "Deliver us from blood-guiltiness, O God," but especially from being guilty of the body and blood of Thy Son.

VERSE 28.

But let a man examine himself, and so let him eat of this bread, and drink of this cup.

LET us know that some make these words, "Let a man examine," to be a bare permission and concession, that if they will they may do it. Others make it a counsel or advice, that according to the rule of prudence or discretion they should do it. A third sort, and that the truest, make it a mandate or command, that we must do it; and the seeming indifferency in the English tongue is necessitated in the Greek, Δοκιμαζέτω.

REASONS OF THE NECESSITY.

1. The first is taken from the majesty of that God to whose presence we approach. Lord, what prodigious state did Ahasuerus, an earthly prince, stand upon! (Esther ii. 12.) The woman that was thought fit to be his wife, must be purified twelve months before, six months with the oil of myrrh, and six months with sweet odours. "Behold, a greater than" Ahasuerus "is here;" and therefore those that come to His table, must seriously examine and prepare themselves before.

2. From the great profit which we receive thereby, if we come prepared.

3. From the grievousness of the punishments, if we be unworthy receivers. The sacrament is not

like to those harmless receipts, (as innocent as the prescribers are simple,) which some good old women give sick people, which, if they do no good, do no harm: but this is a true maxim, "To him to whom the sacrament is not heaven, it is hell." If it brings not profit and spiritual grace, it draws great plagues and punishments on us.

Examine himself.

A Christian's eyes ought to be turned inward, and chiefly reflected on himself: yet how many are there, whose home is to be always abroad! It is a tale of the wandering Jew, but it is too much truth of many wandering Christians, whose thoughts are never resident on their own souls, but ever searching and examining of others. These say not with the soldiers, "And what shall we do?" (Luke iii. 14;) but are questioning always, as St. Peter is of John, "And what shall this man do?" (John xxi. 21.)

Yet a man's examining of himself excludes not his examination of those who are committed to his care and charge; as pastors examining such young people as, according to the orders of the church, they are to catechize. As for that father who trieth his wife and children, he still examineth himself.

Two sorts of people are unfit to receive. 1. Those that wilfully will not examine themselves.

2. Those that cannot, by reason of their want of age, or some other impotency.

Yea, children which are old enough to conceive the words of a minister, yet as yet not of age to partake of the sacrament: think not that the church maketh ciphers of you, and esteemeth you of no account; you are heirs apparent to the sacrament of the Lord's Supper; none can hinder you from it. Yet during your minority the church is your guardian, and carefully keeps that treasure for you, till you come of age, provided you carefully learn your Catechism, to be able to answer your minister. But I will turn my precepts to you into prayers for you, and so "wish you good success in the name of the Lord."

In examining of this word "examine," learned men run in three several streams. Some prosecute the metaphor of a goldsmith, searching the purity of his gold; δοκιμάζειν being a proper word to them in their mystery. 1 Peter i. 7: "Ἵνα τὸ δοκίμιον ὑμῶν τῆς πίστεως πολὺ τιμιώτερον χρυσίου, "That the trial of your faith, being much more precious than of gold that perisheth, though it be tried with fire, might be found unto praise," &c. Others, because bread and wine to be taken in the sacrament are both food and physic, please themselves best to insist on the similitude of a physician, giving preparatives to his patient, before he receives the physic. A third sort make "examine" here to be *verbum forense et juridicum*, as magistrates question offenders; and therefore choose to follow that resemblance. David was in a great strait betwixt three evils; I am in a strait betwixt three goods, not knowing which to choose: however, we will follow the latter, as most consonant to the apostle's sense.

A man, in examining himself, must personate three, and act three several parts. 1. The part of the offender; 2. Of the accuser; 3. Of the judge. The part of the accuser may be well performed by that faculty of the soul which is called "conscience;" for, besides her office to be the register and recorder of the soul, and remembrancer of the acts thereof, it is also the attorney general of the King of Heaven in our hearts, to press the evidence against us after the indictment. As for our reason and judgment, that must supply the office of a judge, *et secundùm allegata et probata* acquit or condemn us.

But here it is to be feared, men will be partial to themselves in two respects. 1. First, in not giving their conscience fair play : they will not give it that liberty Agrippa granted to St. Paul, "Thou art permitted to speak for thyself;" (Acts xxvi. 1;) but what in whole they cannot silence, they will in part disturb and interrupt. 2. It is to be feared our judgment will not be upright; but, as St. Peter said to our Saviour, "Ἵλεώς Σοι, Κύριε,

"Master, spare Thyself," *Propitius Tibi sis* (Matt. xvi. 22,) so our judgment will be partial and favourable to us, as foundered feet will never tread hard.

Wherefore, because of this double suspicion of partiality, this is a sound and safe rule: Let us account ourselves to be worse than upon examination we find ourselves to be. Thus did St. Paul, 1 Cor. iv. 4: "For I know nothing by myself; yet am I not hereby justified: but He that judges me is the Lord." That is, since his conversion, his conscience accused him of no great sin unrepented; and yet hereupon he durst not pronounce himself to be innocent; for "God judgeth not as man judgeth, neither seeth as man seeth;" but those who are acquitted by themselves, may be condemned by Him.

Seeing thus, as it is said, a man is to act three parts, by the way we may observe:

DOCTRINE.

A Christian, though alone, may make company for himself. Psalm iv. 4: "Commune with your hearts in your chamber, and be still." Psalm xliii. 5: "Why art thou so heavy, O my soul? why art thou," &c. One, as we have said, may make himself three,—offender, accuser, judge; so that he should never be less alone than when alone, being always in the company of heavenly discoursers in himself.* Had men the art of these self-examinations and soliloquies, they need not, to put away melancholy, as they pretend, and to avoid solitariness, repair to the schools of drunkenness, there to seek for bad company, that there (to use their own expression) they may drive away the time. Fools, to drive away that which is winged, and which though they should strive to stay, they cannot!

Now the interrogatories, whereupon every man is to be examined, are these.

1. Whether thou dost repair to receive the sacrament with a competent measure of knowledge?

2. Whether dost thou come with unfeigned repentance for thy sins past? which repentance consisteth not so much in outward sorrow (for their faces may be flints, whose hearts may be fountains; their souls may drop blood, whose eyes cannot shed tears) as in the inward contrition and hatred of sin, and shunning of it in the sequel of our lives.

3. Whether dost thou come with a lively faith, relying upon God in Christ for the pardon of thy sins?

4. Whether dost thou come with love undissembled, freely from thy heart to forgive all injuries committed against thee? Some, when they are to partake of the sacrament, say to their

* [Young's lines, near the beginning of "Night the Third," will here recur to some readers:—
"O lost to virtue, lost to manly thought,
Lost to the noble sallies of the soul,
Who think it solitude to be alone!" &c.—ED.]

malice, as Abraham did to his two servants, "Abide you here; and I will go yonder, and worship, and come again to you." (Gen. xxii. 5.) They leave their injuries at the church door, till they have received the Lord's supper, and then returning make a resumption of them again. But let us not only lop the boughs, but grub up even the roots, of our malice; not only suspend the act, but depose the habit, of our hatred.

And here, as God said to the Jews, (Ezek. xviii. 3,) that they should have no occasion any more to use that proverb in Israel, "The fathers have eaten sour grapes, and the children's teeth are set on edge;" in like manner I could wish no occasion that the English by-word be any more used, "I forgive him, but I will not forget him." Such people, I dare say, neither forgive nor forget; like sluts, they sweep the house of their heart, but leave all the dust still behind the door. But let us not only break the teeth of our malice in forgiving, but also pluck out the sting, which is still behind in the tail, and labour fully to forget.

To these interrogatories some have added these additionals, which virtually are contained in the former:—Whether dost thou come with an earnest desire and longing to be made partaker of these heavenly mysteries? Whether dost thou come with thankfulness to the God of heaven for this His great blessing?

Hereon let every one examine himself. I dare boldly say, none can decline the answering to these interrogatories: not that common evasion, *Non tenetur respondere*, as if they were not absolutely pertinent to the matter in hand; but it concerns every one of us to make a punctual and direct answer thereunto.

Upon examination all will confess themselves guilty, except a dumb devil or a pharisaical spirit hath possessed any. Yet are there degrees of guiltiness. Some are guilty that they have not these graces at all, but the opposite vices instead of them; instead of knowledge, ignorance. All the reason Laban could render Jacob in cozening him with the elder sister for the younger, was but pleading the custom of the country. (Gen. xxix. 26.) And this is the best account some can give, why they receive the sacrament: it is an old ceremony, a fashion of their forefathers, a custom of the church, that young men and maidens at such an age use to receive. And so of the rest: instead of repentance, obstinacy in sin; in lieu of faith, unbelief; in place of charity, malice; an indifferency for desire, and ingratitude for thankfulness. These in no case must presume to receive, but tarry till these vices are amended, and graces in some degree begotten in them.

Others are guilty, that though they have them in sincerity, yet they have them not in perfection.

These are bound to come to God's table; His dainties are provided properly for such guests; and by His blessing these holy mysteries may work in them what is wanting, and strengthen what is weak. And, to conclude, as the father of the lunatic child cried out, "Lord, I believe; help my unbelief;" (Mark ix. 24;) so may the best of us all, when we come to communicate, call out with tears, "Lord, I come with knowledge; help my want of knowledge: Lord, I come with repentance; help my want of repentance: Lord, I come with faith; help my want of faith: Lord, I come with love; help my want of love: Lord, I come," &c.

VERSE 30.

For this cause many are weak and sick among you, and many sleep.

RIGHT at this time there raged and reigned in the church of Corinth an epidemical disease; and my apostle in my text tells them the fountain from which it flowed; namely, from the unprepared and unreverent receiving of the sacrament. The words contain the punishment, and the cause thereof. I must confess, in the heraldry of nature, the cause is to be handled before the effect; but because the punishment, being the effect, discovered itself first, while the cause was yet unknown, we will first treat thereof. The punishment contains three steps to the grave:

1. Weakness. 2. Sickness. 3. Temporal death; called "sleep." Learn,

God inflicteth not the same punishment for all, but hath variety of correction. In His quiver some arrows are blunt, some sharp; and of these some He draws half-way, some to the head. And the reason is, because there are divers degrees of men's sins: some sin out of ignorance, others out of knowledge; some out of infirmity, others of presumption; some once, others often; some at the seducing of others, others seduce others. God therefore doth not like the unskilful empirics, who prescribe the same quantity of the same receipt at all times, to all ages, tempers, and diseases. But wisely He varieth His physic,—"few stripes" to those that knew not His will, and "many stripes" for them who knew His will, and did it not. Sometimes He shooteth half cannon,—weakness; sometimes full cannon,—sickness; sometimes murdering pieces,—death itself. *

USE I.

Let us endeavour to amend, when God layeth His least judgment upon us. Let us humble

* [The different sizes of cannon were formerly distinguished as "whole" or "full cannon," "half" or "demi cannon," &c.;—"murdering pieces," according to Phillips, ("New World of Words,") being "small cannon, either of brass or iron, having a chamber or charge, consisting of nails, old iron, &c., put in at their breech,"—the comparatively harmless fore-runners of the "Armstrongs," &c., of the present day.—ED.]

ourselves with true repentance under His hand when He layeth His "little finger" upon us, lest we cause Him to lay His "loins" on us : let us be bettered when He scourgeth us "with rods," lest we give Him occasion to sting us "with scorpions;" for light punishments, neglected, will draw heavier upon us.

USE II.

Let magistrates and men in authority mitigate or increase the punishment, according to the nature of the offence. Let there be as well the stocks for the drunkard, the house of correction for the idle drone, the whip for the petty lassoner,* as the brand for the felon, and the gallows for the murderer. Let mercy improve itself, to obtain, if not a pardon, yet a lighter punishment for those in whose faces are read the performance of present sorrow, and promise of future amendment. Let severity lay load on their backs which are old and incorrigible sinners, so that there is more fear of their perverting others than hope of their converting. Then shall the gods in earth be like to the God in heaven, and magistrates here imitate the pattern which God setteth in my text. For probable it is that those Corinthians who are least offenders in the irreverent receiving of the sacrament, were

* [A mis-spelling for "larcener," *i. e.*, thief. The term is now obsolete in both spellings.—ED.]

punished with weakness; the greater, with sickness; the greatest of all, with death temporal, called "sleep" in my text.

The death of the godly in Scripture language is often styled "sleep." And indeed Sleep and Death are two twins: Sleep is the elder brother, for Adam slept in paradise; but Death liveth longest, for "the last enemy that shall be destroyed is Death." But some will object, "Was St. Paul so charitably opinioned to these Corinthians, as to think that they, some whereof were drunken at the receiving of the sacrament,—that they 'slept;' that is, died and went to heaven? Methinks so strong a charity argues too weak a judgment." I answer, the apostle had perceived in these men's lives the strength of unfeigned piety; and though God suffered them to fall into a sin of so high a nature as this must be confessed to be, yet St. Paul did Christianly believe that this sin, by repentance and faith in Christ, was pardoned, and their souls eternally saved. Let us measure the estates of men after death by the rule of their lives; and though we see some commit grievous sins, yea, such sins for which they are brought to exemplary death, (perchance by the orderly proceeding of the law,) yet withal, if we had known that the drift and scope of their lives had been to fear God, we may and must charitably conceive of their final estate, and that, with the

Corinthians in my text, they are fallen asleep. So much for the punishment: we come now to the cause: "For this cause many are weak."

All sicknesses of the body proceed from the sin of the soul. I am not ignorant that the lethargy ariseth from the coldness of the brain; that the dropsy floweth from waterish blood in an ill-affected liver; that the spleen is caused from melancholy wind, gathered in the midriff: but the cause of all these causes, the fountain of all these fountains, is the sin of the soul. And not only the sins which we have lately committed, and [which] still lie fresh bleeding on our consciences, but even those which we have committed long ago, and which process of time hath since scarred over. Job xiii. 26: "For thou writest bitter things against me, and makest me possess the sins of my youth." So that Job being grey is punished for Job being green; Job in the autumn of his age smarts for what he hath done in the spring of his age: and as those which have been given to violent exercises in their youth, when they are old, read the admonitions of their former folly in the aches of their bones; so they who have prodigally rioted their youth out in vicious courses, in their old age find the smart of it in their weak and diseased bodies. Do we then desire to lead our old age in health, I know no better preservative or diet drink can be prescribed than in our youth to keep our souls from sin; for now we sow the seeds of health or sickness, which perchance we shall reap twenty years after.

QUESTION.

But how came St. Paul to know that this sickness of the Corinthians proceeded from the irreverent receiving of the sacrament, especially sithence [since] there were four other grand sins which then reigned in their church, each whereof, upon hue and cry, might be taken as suspicious to be the cause of this disease? 1. Factious affecting of one minister above another, to the disgrace of God and the Gospel. 1 Corinthians i. 12: "Now this I say, that every one of you saith, I am of Paul; I am of Apollos; I am of Cephas; and I am of Christ." 2. Suffering an "incestuous person," husband to his mother, and son to his wife, to live amongst them without public penance and punishment. For though this incest, as it was committed but by one man, was but a particular and personal sin, yet as it was connived at, and not punished, it began gangrene-like to spread, and, leaving its nature of personality, it entituled itself to be a public, general, church sin of the Corinthians. 3. Going to law one with another under heathen judges. 1 Cor. vi. 1: "Dare any of you, having business against another, be judged by the unjust, and not by the saints?" 4. Denying the resurrection of the body. 1 Cor. xv. 12:

"How say some among you that there is no resurrection of the dead?" Sithence [since] therefore at the same time the Corinthians were guilty of factious affecting of their ministers, going to law under pagan judges, suffering an incestuous person to live amongst them unpunished, denying of the resurrection of the body; why might not St. Paul think that any one or all of these might be the cause of this disease in the church of Corinth, as well as the irreverent receiving of the sacrament?

ANSWER I.

Because this sin was the sin paramount, like Saul, "higher than his fellows, from the shoulders upwards." The other four sins were felony, robbing God of His glory; but the irreverent receiving of the sacrament was high treason against the person of Christ, and so against God Himself. The other four sins were tetrarchs reigning over the Corinthians; but this was as Augustus the emperor over the tetrarchs, more conspicuous than any of the rest. Learn we, then, that though God of His goodness may be pleased graciously to pardon and pass by sins of an inferior nature and meaner alloy, yet He will not hold them guiltless, and let them escape unpunished, who irreverently receive the body and blood of His Son. This Stentor sin shouts in God's ears for revenge. St. Anselm saith, that many diseases that reign in the summer, (though physicians may impute them to other second causes,) proceed from people's irreverent receiving the sacrament at Easter.

ANSWER II.

Because the apostle perceived some resemblance betwixt the sin committed and the punishment inflicted. For, as a physician, when he comes to his patient, and finds him strangely affected, so that the disease puzzles all his rules of art to reduce it to some natural cause, then he will be ready to suspect that his patient hath eaten some poison, which hath strangely envenomed the estate of his body; so St. Paul, seeing the Corinthians to be punished with a strange and unusual sickness, (some conceive it was the plague,) presently suspected that they had eaten some poisonous thing, and on inquiry he finds that it was the sacrament irreverently received: it being just with God to turn that which was appointed to be preservative for the soul, to prove poison to the body, being not received with due preparation. And here I may adventure upon a profitable discourse, how a man in his sickness may come to know the very particular sin for which God hath inflicted that sickness upon him. It is not a mere curiosity, which will afford the groundwork of much good meditation; nor an impossibility, though a difficulty to arrive at the knowledge of it. Wherefore let a man in such a case summon all his great sins to make a personal appearance in his memory; and not only those of the last edition, but even those whose impression is almost out of the date of his memory, such as were committed long ago in his youth. This done, all the matter will be to find out which is the veriest sin for which God punisheth him at that time: and here I must confess my candles to be but dim; but I will light the more of them.

REASONS.

1. First, see to which sin the punishment thou sufferest, bears the most proportion of resemblance; for God commonly punisheth like with the like. Thus one may see God's hand in the cutting off one of Adoni-bezek's fingers, he being served as he had served seventy-two kings. And thus King Jehoram, who had cruelly slaughtered his brethren on a stone, was troubled with an incurable disease, that his bowels fell out: and just it was that he should have no bowels, that had no compassion.

2. See if thou canst not find some proportion in the disproportion, and likeness in the unlikeness, of some sin to this punishment; God ofttimes punishing by the contrary. Thus those who, out of niceness and curiosity, have took more than comes to the share of a corrupt creature, are commonly sent to their graves by some nasty and loathsome disease; as proud Herod, whom the

worms, impatient to stay so long till death had dished him for their palate, devoured him alive.

3. Something may be gathered from the place or part wherein the disease lieth. For, if it be in the eyes, it is probable it is inflicted for the shooting out of lustful and lascivious glances, or looking with envious and covetous sight on the means of others. If in the ears, for giving audience to wanton sonnets, or for being over credulous in the hearing ill reports of others. If in the tongue, for lying, swearing, &c.

4. See whether chronology, or the time wherein the sickness seizeth upon thee, will not something advantage thee for the discovering the cause thereof. Thus, as one observes, the Lord Hastings was beheaded at London that very self-same day twelvemonth, yea, the same hour, and, if curiosity may go further, the same minute, wherein he had conspired the death of the queen's kindred at Pomfret Castle.

5. Consider what sin it is, for the committing whereof thou hast conceived the least sorrow. For though we can never be condignly sorry for our least sin, yet we may be more penitent for one sin than for another; and that sin which hath cost us the slightest and shallowest repentance, is most likely to be the cause of our present sickness.

6. Hearken chiefly to the indictment of thy conscience. For, when we hunt after that sin

which causeth our disease, and we find ourselves to be either at a loss, or at a cold scent, if once our conscience begin to spend her open mouth, we may certainly conclude that the game went that way, and that that is the very sin for which at that time we are punished. Thus the patriarchs, Gen. xlii. 21, "said one to another, We have verily sinned against our brother, in that we saw the anguish of his soul, when he besought us, and we would not hear; therefore is this evil fallen upon us." Reuben did not impute it to the defiling of his father's bed, nor Judah to his incest, nor Simeon and Levi to their murdering of the Shechemites; for these were but personal sins: but all jointly agreed that it was for their cruelty to their brother, a sin wherein all they were equally engaged, as they were equally inwrapt in the punishment.

If by these or any other means we attain to the knowledge of that particular sin for which we are punished, let us drown that sin in penitent tears, and in the blood of our Saviour. But if we cannot find it out, let us imitate the example of Herod, (Matt. ii.,) who, that he might make sure work to kill our Saviour, slew all the children in Bethlehem and the country about it, from two years old and under; a plot probable to have taken effect, if Heaven had not been too wise for hell. In like manner, let us indifferently and impartially repent for all our sins in general: if we know not which was the bee that stung us, let us throw down the whole hive; if we know not which was the thorn that pricked us, let us cut down the whole hedge, and so we shall be sure that sin shall not escape, which hath caused our present sickness.

Now, whereas God might have tumbled the Corinthians down into hell-fire, for their irreverent receiving of the sacrament, and yet was pleased to inflict on them bodily weakness and sickness, and death, we learn,—

God oftentimes with His saints commuteth eternal torments into temporal punishments. He is therefore angry in this world, that He might not be angry in the world to come, *et misericorditer adhibet temporalem pœnam, ne justè inferat æternam ultionem.* If any object, "But why will God pardon talents, and not tokens; pounds, but not pence; and for Christ's sake forgive and strike off eternal torment, and yet not cross the score of temporal punishment?" I answer, 1. To make us take notice that we have been offenders. 2. That, by feeling the smart of what He inflicteth on us, we may be the more sensible of His favour, how much pain He hath forgiven us. 3. To make us more wary and watchful in time to come. But far be it from us to conceive that there is any satisfactory or expiatory power in the afflictions which we suffer. Satisfaction for sin could not be but once; and once was fully made, when Christ offered Himself upon the cross.

USE.

Let us therefore learn patience under God's afflicting hand, when He layeth any sickness upon us. Solomon said to Abiathar, (1 Kings ii. 26,) "Get thee to Anathoth, to thine own fields; for thou art worthy of death: but I will not at this time put thee to death, because thou barest the ark of my Lord God before David my father." Thus God dealeth with us, when He might justly deprive us of our life, yea, of our eternal life; yet if we have borne His ark, if we can plead any true reference or relation to Christ our Saviour, God will be graciously pleased, not to take away our lives, but only to send us to our Anathoth, to confine us to our beds, to keep us His close prisoners, and only to deprive us of our health, pleasure, and delight. Let us therefore patiently endure the aching of the teeth; we have all deserved the gnashing of the teeth. Let us patiently endure a burning fever; for we have all deserved hell fire. Let us patiently endure a bodily consumption; for we have deserved to be consumed, and brought to nothing.

GROWTH IN GRACE.

2 PETER III. 18:

But grow in grace, and in the knowledge of our Lord and Saviour Jesus Christ.

1. PHILOSOPHERS make a double growth. One, *per aggregationem materiæ*, "by gaining of more matter." Thus rivers grow by the accession of tributary brooks; heaps of corn wax greater by the addition of more grain; and thus stones grow, as some would have it, though this more properly be termed an augmentation, or increase, than a growth. The other, *per intro-receptionem nutrimenti*, "by receiving of nourishment within," as plants, beasts, and men grow. Of the latter growth we understand the apostle in the text, and will prosecute the metaphor of the growth of vegetables, as that which the Holy Spirit seems most to favour and intend in these expressions.

2. Here is one thing presupposed in the text, and laid down for a foundation; namely, that

those to whom St. Peter writes were already rooted in grace and goodness. There must be an unit at least, before any multiplication; a basis, before any building upon it. No doubt they were such as to whom St. Paul writes, Eph. iii. 17, ἐν ἀγάπῃ ἐρριζωμένοι, "being rooted and grounded in love;" such as the Colossians were, Col. ii. 7, "rooted in Christ, and established in faith." And such I trust you are, to whom my discourse is directed; or else it were in vain for me, or any, to give you instructions for *growth in grace*.

OBJECTION.

3. But why is it said in the text, first "in grace," and then "in knowledge?" This seems to be an ὕστερον προτερόν. The lantern is to go first; knowledge is to be the usher of grace; information in the understanding must go before reformation in the will and affections.

ANSWER.

I could answer, The Holy Spirit is no whit curious in marshalling these graces, which He putteth first; they need no herald to show their pedigree, which will not fall out for precedency. But to the point: there is a twofold knowledge: one precedent grace, as disposing one thereto, and making capable thereof; the other subsequent, and is an effect thereof, and a reward of it through God's mercy. These that have gracious hearts do daily better and improve their knowledge in matters of salvation; and some herein arrive at a great height; as David, Psalm cxix. 99: "I have more understanding than all my teachers: for Thy testimonies are my meditations."

4. However, see, the apostle puts grace and knowledge together. "What God hath joined, let no man put asunder." We must grow according to both dimensions, both in height, in knowledge, and in breadth, in piety; both in head and in heart; both in speculation and practice. We must not all run up in height, like a hop-pole, but also burnish * and spread in breadth: then shall we be well proportioned and complete. And, indeed, practice without knowledge is blind, and knowledge without practice is lame.

5. Three things are required to make a plant to grow. First, That it hath life within it. Thus the Christian must have in his soul a quickening, vivifying faith. Secondly, It must be watered in a man with the dew of God's word, Isaiah lv. 10: "For as the rain cometh down, and the snow from heaven, and returneth not thither, but watereth the earth, and maketh it bring forth and bud, that it may give seed to the sower, and bread to the eater; so shall My word be that goeth forth out of My mouth," &c. And the same allegory is followed by Moses, Deut. xxxii. 2: "My doctrine

* [In the obsolete sense, " grow or spread out."—ED.]

shall drop as the rain, my speech shall distil as the dew, as the small rain upon the tender herb, and as the showers upon the grass." Thirdly, The blessing of God is requisite, without which both the former are nothing worth. Paul may "plant," and Apollos may "water; but God giveth the increase." It was observed of Master Greenham, that painful and zealous preacher of God's word, that, though he was very industrious in his calling, yet his people still remained most ignorant; and, as one saith,

"Greenham had pastures green,
But sheep full lean."

So true it is, that God's blessing is the key of the work, without which all is but labour in vain.

6. Now we may take notice of two remarkables in the growth of a Christian. First, Plants have their ἀκμή, their bounds, both in height and breadth, set by nature; ("Hither shalt thou come, and no further;") to which when they have attained, they grow downward and wax less. Yea, all sublunary things *habent suos terminos, quò cùm venerint sistunt, retrocedunt, ruunt.* But *growth in grace* admits of no such period, but still there is *plus ultra.* What St. Paul saith, "Pray continually; rejoice evermore," (1 Thess. v. 17,) is as true of spiritual growth: grow continually; increase evermore; never stop nor stay in grace, till thou

comest to glory. Secondly, Trees dote, as well as men, in their old age; yea, then they are barren, and bring forth little or no fruit: whereas Christians, on the contrary, "that be planted in the house of the Lord, shall flourish in the court of our God. They shall still bring forth fruit in old age; they shall be fat and flourishing." (Psalm xcii. 13, 14.) Like wine, they are best when they are oldest; like Caleb, able and active men, even at fourscore years of age.

7. Come we now to set down those things which do either in part hinder, or in whole destroy, men's growth in grace. For the first, let us take heed of *suckers* in our soul; such superfluous excremental sprigs which, like so many thieves, steal away the nourishment which should maintain the tree. By these "suckers" we may understand those felonious avocations of worldly employments, which either out of season, or out of measure, busy our souls in earthly things, when they should be employed in heavenly matters. The only way to prevent this mischief is to prune and cut off these suckers, and speedily to stop up these emissaries, by outlets and private sluices, lest they drain dry the very main channel of grace in our hearts.

8. As for destroyers of grace, it is twofold. First, the blighting or blasting of a conscience-wasting sin. Thus drunkenness and incest destroyed grace in Lot for that very instant, till he

recovered himself again by unfeigned repentance. Secondly, the drowth [drought] and scorching heat of persecution. How promising a plant! what a shoot in goodness did he give on a sudden, who said to our Saviour, "Master, I will follow Thee whithersoever Thou goest!" But how quickly was he withered with one scorching beam, when Christ told him how hard service he must undergo!

9. Observe by the way: there is a double rooting in grace,—the one a sound and sure one, the other but shallow and superficial. The former rooting belongs to the saints of God; and these, though they may be blighted with sin, or scorched with persecution, yet still, as I may say, there is a secret sprig of life in the root, though in outward appearance the leaves and boughs may seem quite dead; and in God's due time they grow out of their sins by repentance, out of their afflictions by patience. Let us therefore take heed of being too tyrannical, in passing sentence of condemnation upon them before the time. Scotus, that famous schoolman, being in a strong fit of an apoplexy, was, by the cruel kindness of his over-officious friends, buried before he was dead.* Many, overhasty in their uncharitable censures, seeing one fallen into a sin, bury him alive in their judgments, counting him a castaway and reprobate, when by

---

* Camden's "Britannia," in Northumberland.

God's mercy and his own repentance he may recover again, as still retaining in his heart some sparks of spiritual life. As for the wicked, which have only a superficial hold in grace, rather sticked than rooted in it; we see what our Saviour saith of them: "And forthwith they sprung up, because they had no deepness of earth: and when the sun was up, they were scorched: and because they had not root, they withered away." They were quite dried up, and here made fuel for hell, never recovering themselves any more; whereas the godly, though they seem dead in the winter, they may grow again next spring.

USE.

· 10. This doctrine, if applied, serves to confute many. First, those that grow backward in grace, and are worse now than they were seven years before; like the Galatians, "You have run well; who hindered you?" Secondly, those who stand still in goodness; like those women whereof the apostle complaineth, that they were "ever learning, and never come to the knowledge of the truth." Thirdly, those that grow, but not proportionably to the long time wherein they have been planted, the fat soil wherein they have been set. (1.) The long time wherein they have been planted: "For when for the time ye ought to be teachers, you have need that one teach you again which be the first principles of the oracles of God; and are become such as have need of milk, and not of strong meat." (Heb. v. 12.) (2.) The fatness of the soil wherein they have been set, and plenty of water poured on them: and herein no country comes near to ours; and therefore we are most unexcusable, if we grow not in grace. Outlandish men call our land "the rainy land," because we have such plenty thereof, arising of the store of vapours, from the vicinity of the sea. They call it also "the ringing island," because it hath bells, so many and so tuneable. I am sure, without flattering, it may be thus called in a higher sense: the dew of God's word is nowhere poured more plentifully; and we have (God increase their number!) many and melodious bells, tuneable amongst themselves, and loud-sounding the word of God to others. Most heavy, therefore, will be our account, if we yield not some proportionable growth in grace to these great means God affords us.

11. Now, in examining themselves, I find three sorts of men to be deceived. Some account themselves to be grown in grace, when they are not: others esteem themselves to be not grown, when they are. Of the former, some account themselves to be improved in goodness, when God takes from them the ability to commit sin they had formerly. An old man saith, "I thank God I am grown in grace." Well, how shall this appear? "Thus," saith the old man: "twenty years ago I was given

to lust and wantonness; now I have left it." Alas! he puts a fallacy on his own soul; for the sin hath left him, his moisture is spent, his heat abated, and he disabled from performing the task of wickedness. So the prodigal, who hath spent his estate, hugs himself in his own happiness, that now he is grown in grace, because he hath left vanity in clothes, curiosity in diet, excessiveness in gaming; when, alas! needs must the fire go out, when the fuel is taken away; he is not grown in grace, but decreased in estate. Others construe it to be growth of grace in themselves, when only God takes away from them the temptations to sin. He that, living in a populous place, was given to drunkenness, who now, being retired to a private village, takes himself to be turned very sober:—alas! it is not he that is altered, but his place. He wanteth now (a want with gain) a crew of bad good-fellows to solicit him to the tavern; but, had he the same temptation, let him examine himself, whether he would not be as bad as ever he was before.

A third sort count themselves grown in grace, when they have not left, but only exchanged, their sin; and perchance a less for a greater. "Thou that abhorrest idols, committest thou sacrilege?" (Rom. ii. 22.) Some think themselves improved in piety, because they left prodigality, and reel into covetousness; left profaneness, and [have] fallen into spiritual pride, or peevish affecting of outside holiness. Thus, like the sea, what they lose in one place, they gain in another, and are no whit grown in grace.

12. Others conceive themselves not to be grown in grace when they are grown; and that in these four cases. (1.) First, Sometimes they think that they have less grace now than they had seven years ago; because they are more sensible of their badness. They daily see, and grieve to see, how spiritual the law of God is, and how carnal they are; how they sin both against God's will and their own, and sorrow after their sin, and sin after their sorrow. This makes many mistake themselves to be worse than they have been formerly; whereas, indeed, the sick man begins to amend, when he begins to feel his pain.

13. (2.) Many think themselves to have less saving knowledge now than they had at their first conversion; both because (as we said before of grace) they are now more sensible of their ignorance; and because their knowledge at their first conversion seemed a great deal, which since seemeth not increased, because increased insensibly and by unappearing degrees. One that hath lived all his life-time in a most dark dungeon, and at last is brought out but into the twilight, more admires at the clearness and brightness thereof, than he will wonder a month after at the sun at

noonday. So a Christian newly regenerated, and brought out of the dark state of nature into the life of grace, is more apprehensive, at the first illumination, of the knowledge he receives, than of far greater degrees of knowledge which he receiveth afterwards.

14. (3.) Some think they have less grace now than they had some years since, because a great measure of grace seems but little to him that desires more. As, in worldly wealth, *crescit amor nummi quantum ipsa pecunia crescit;* so is there a holy, heavenly, and laudable covetousness of grace, which deceives the eye of the soul, and makes a great deal of goodness seem but a little.

15. (4.) Many think they are grown less and weaker in grace, when indeed they are assaulted with stronger temptations. One saith, " Seven years since, I vanquished such temptations as at this day foil me; therefore surely I am decreased in grace." *Non sequitur;* for, though it be the same temptation in kind, it may not be the same in degree and strength; thou mayest still be as valiant, yet thy enemies may conquer thee, as assaulting thee with more force and fury. When thou wert newly converted, God proportioned the weight to the weakness of thy shoulders; bound up the devil, that he should set upon thee with no more force than thou couldest resist and subdue. Now thou hast gotten a greater stock of grace, God

suffers the devil to buffet thee with greater blows.

16. (5.) Some think grace is less in them now than it was at their first conversion, because they find not in their souls such violent flashes, such strong, impetuous,—I had almost said, furious,—raptures of goodness, and flashes of grace and heavenly illumination. But let them seriously consider, that these raptures which they then had, and now complain they want, were but fits short and sudden,—*Nimbus erat, citò præteriit,*—not settled and constant, but such as quickly spent themselves with their own violence: whereas grace in them now may be more solid, reduced, digested, and concocted;—*Bos lassus fortiùs figit pedem;*—more slow, but more sure; less violent, but more constant. Though grace be not so thick at one time, yet now it is beaten and hammered out to be broader and longer; yea, I might add also, it is more pure and refined. This we may see in St. Peter: when he was a young man, in a bravery, he would walk on the water; yea, and so daring was he in his promises: "Though all forsake Thee, yet will not I:" but afterwards in his old age he was not so bold and daring; experience had not only corrected the rankness of his spirit, but also in some sort quenched, surely tempered, the flashes of his zeal for the adventurousness of it. Yet was he never a whit the

worse, but the better, Christian : though he was not so quick to run into danger, yet he would answer the spur, when need required, and not flinch for persecution, when just occasion was offered; as at last he suffered martyrdom gloriously for Christ.

17. To conclude : grace in the good thief on the cross, like Jonah's gourd, grew up presently; for he was an extraordinary example: but in us it is like the growth of an oak, slow and insensible; so that we may sooner find it *crevisse*, than *crescere*. It must therefore be our daily task all the days of our lives : to which end let us remember to pray to God for His blessing on us. Our Saviour saith, " Which of you by taking care is able to add one cubit unto his stature " in the corporal growth ? (Matt. vi. 27.) Much less able are we in the spiritual growth to add one inch or hair's breadth to the height of our souls. Then, what was pride in the builders of Babel will be piety in us,—to mount and raise our souls so high, till the top of them shall reach to heaven. Amen.

HOW FAR EXAMPLES ARE TO BE FOLLOWED.

RUTH I. 15:

And Naomi said, Behold, thy sister-in-law is gone back unto her people, and unto her gods: return thou after thy sister-in-law.

IN these words Naomi seeks to persuade Ruth to return, alleging the example of Orpah, who, as she saith, was "gone back to her people, and to her gods." Where, first, we find that all the heathen, and the Moabites amongst the rest, did not acknowledge one true God, but were the worshippers of many gods; for they made every attribute of God to be a distinct deity. Thus, instead of that attribute, the wisdom of God, they feigned Apollo the god of wisdom; instead of the power of God, they made Mars the god of power; instead of that admirable beauty of God, they had Venus the goddess of beauty. But no one attribute was so much abused as God's providence. For the heathen supposing that the whole world, and all the creatures therein, was too great a diocese to be daily visited by one and the same Deity, they therefore assigned sundry gods to several creatures. Thus God's providence in ruling the raging of the seas was counted Neptune; in stilling the roaring wind, Æolus; in commanding the powers of hell, Pluto; yea, sheep had their Pan, and gardens their Pomona; the heathens then being as fruitful in feigning of gods, as the Papists since in making of saints.

Now, because Naomi used the example of Orpah as a motive to work upon Ruth to return, we gather from thence, examples of others set before our eyes are very potent and prevailing arguments, to make us follow and imitate them; whether they be good examples,—so the forwardness of the Corinthians to relieve the Jews provoked many,—or whether they be bad,—so the dissembling of Peter at Antioch drew Barnabas. and others into the same fault. But those examples, of all others, are most forcible with us, which are set by such who are near to us by kindred, or gracious with us in friendship, or great over us in power.

Let men in eminent places, as magistrates, ministers, fathers, masters, (so that others love to dance after their pipe, to sing after their music, to tread after their track,) endeavour to propound themselves examples of piety and religion to those that be under them.

When we see any good example propounded unto us, let us strive with all possible speed to imitate it. What a deal of stir is there in the world for civil precedency and priority! Every one desires to march in the forefront, and thinks it a shame to come lagging in the rearward. O that there were such a holy ambition and heavenly emulation in our hearts, that, as Peter and John ran a race, who should come first to the grave of our Saviour, so men would contend, who should first attain to true mortification. And when we see a good example set before us, let us imitate it, though it be in one which in outward respects is far our inferior. Shall not our masters be ashamed, to see that their men, whose place on earth is to come behind them, in piety towards heaven go before them? Shall not the husband blush to see his wife, which is the weaker vessel in nature, the stronger vessel in grace? Shall not the elder brother dye his cheeks with the colour of virtue, to see his younger brother, who was last born, first reborn by faith and the Holy Ghost? Yet let him not therefore envy his brother, as Cain did Abel; let him not be angry with his brother, because he is better than himself; but let him be angry with himself, because he is worse than his brother; let him turn all his malice into imitation, all his fretting at him into following of him. Say unto him, as Gehazi did of Naaman,

"As the Lord liveth, I will run after him:" and although thou canst not over-run him, nor as yet over-look him; yet give not over to run with him, follow him, though not as Asahel did Abner, hard at the heels; yet, as Peter did our Saviour, "afar off;" that though the more slowly, yet as surely thou mayest come to heaven; and though thou wert short of him while he lived, in the race, yet thou shalt be even with him when thou art dead, at the mark.

When any bad example is presented unto us, let us decline and detest it, though the men be never so many, or so dear unto us. Imitate Micaiah, (1 Kings xxii.,) to whom when the messenger sent to fetch him said, "Behold now, the words of the prophets declare good unto the king with one mouth: let thy word therefore, I pray thee, be like to one of them;" Micaiah answered, "As the Lord liveth, whatsoever the Lord saith unto me, that will I speak." If they be never so dear unto us, we must not follow their bad practice. So must the son please him that begot him, that he doth not displease Him that created him: so must the wife follow him that married her, that she doth not offend Him that made her. Wherefore, as Samson, though bound with new cords, snapped them asunder, as tow when it feeleth the fire; so, rather than we should be led by the lewd examples of those that be near and dear unto us, let us break in pieces all their engagements, relations whatsoever.

Now here it will be a labour-worthy discourse, to consider how far the examples even of good men in the Bible are to be followed. For, as all examples have a great influence on the practice of the beholders, so especially the deeds of good men registered in the Scripture (the calendar of eternity) are most attractive of imitation.

FIRST KIND OF EXAMPLES.

We find in Holy Writ nine several kinds of examples. First, *actions extraordinary*, the doers whereof had peculiar strength and dispensation from God to do them. Thus, Phinehas in a heavenly fury killed Cozbi and Zimri; Samson slew himself and the Philistines in the temple of Dagon; Elias caused fire to descend on the two captains of fifties; Elisha cursed the children, the children of Bethel.

USE OF THEM.

These are written for our instruction, not for our imitation. If, with Elisha, thou canst make a bridge over Jordan with thy cloak, if, with him, thou canst raise dead children, then it is lawful for thee, with Elisha, to curse thy enemies. If thou canst not imitate him in the one, pretend not to follow him in the other.

ABUSE OF THEM.

When men propound such examples for their

practice, what is said is imputed to Phinehas for righteousness will be imputed to us for iniquity, if, being private men, by a commission of our own penning, we usurp the sword of justice to punish malefactors.

SECOND SORT.

Actions founded in the ceremonial law : as, Abraham's circumcising of Isaac, Hezekiah's eating the passover, Solomon's offering of sacrifices, &c.

USE OF THEM.

We are to be thankful to God, that these shadows in Christ the substance are taken away. Let us not therefore superstitiously feign that the ghosts of these ceremonies may still walk, which long since were buried in Christ's grave.

ABUSE OF THEM.

By those who still retain them. Excellently Ignatius, *Epist. ad Magnesios*, Οὐ γὰρ Χριστιανισμὸς οὐκ ἔστιν 'Ιουδαϊσμός. Yea, we must forfeit the name of Christians, if we still retain such old rites. Let those who are admitted in the college of grace, disdain any longer to go to the school of the ceremonial law, which truly may be called "the school of Tyrannus."

THIRD SORT.

Actions which are founded in the judicial law; as, punishing theft with fourfold restitution, putting of adulterers to death, and raising up seed to the brother, &c.

USE OF THEM.

These oblige men to observe them so far as they have in them any taste or tincture of a moral law; and as they bear proportion with those statutes by which every particular country is governed. For the judicial law was by God calculated alone for the elevation of the Jewish commonwealth. It suited only with the body of their state; and will not fit any other commonwealth, except it be equal to Judea in all dimensions. I mean, in climate, nature of the soil, disposition of the people, quality of the bordering neighbours, and many other particulars, amongst which the very least is considerable.

ABUSE OF THEM.

When men, out of an over-imitativeness of holy precedents, seek to conform all countries to Jewish laws. That must needs break, which is stretched further than God intended it. They may sooner make Saul's armour fit David, and David's sling and scrip become Saul, than the particular statutes of one country adequately to comply with another.

FOURTH SORT.

Actions founded in no law at all, but only in an ancient custom, by God winked and connived at; yea, tolerated, at the leastwise not openly forbidden in precept, or punished in practice. As polygamy, in the patriarchs having many wives. Indeed, when God first made the large volume of the world, and all creatures therein, and set it forth, *cum regali privilegio*, " Behold, all things therein were very good," He made one Eve for one Adam. Polygamy is an *erratum*, and needs an *Index expurgatorius*, being crept in, being more than what was in the maiden copy: it was the creature of Lamech, no work of God.

USE.

We are herein to wonder at and praise the goodness of God, who was pleased herein to wink at the faults of His dear saints, and to pass by their frailty herein, because they lived in a dark age, wherein His pleasure was not so plainly manifested.

ABUSE OF THEM.

If any, in this bright sunshine of the Gospel, pretend, as a plea for their lust, to follow their example.

FIFTH SORT.

Doubtful examples; which may be so termed, because it is difficult to decide whether the actors of them therein did offend or no; so that, should a jury of learned writers be empanneled to pass their verdict upon them, they would be puzzled whether to condemn or acquit them, and at last be forced to find it an *Ignoramus*. As, whether David did well to dissemble himself frantic, thereby to escape the cruelty of Achish, king of

Gath :—whether Hushai did well in counterfeiting with Absalom, or whether therein he did not make heaven to bow too much to earth; I mean, policy to intrench upon piety; and so in this act was so good a statesman that he was a bad man.

USE OF THEM.

Let us not meddle with imitation of these actions, that are so full of difficulty and danger that our judgments therein may easily be deceived. The sons of Barzillai, (Ezra ii. 63,) because their genealogies were doubtful and uncertain, were put by the priesthood, till a priest should rise up " with Urim and Thummim; " by which we may understand some especial man amongst them, who by God's Spirit might be able to decide the controversies which were questioned in their pedigrees. So let us refrain from following these doubtful examples, till (which in this world is not likely to be) there arise an infallible judge, which can determine in these particulars, whether these actions were well done or no.

ABUSE OF THEM.

By such who, though they have room enough besides, yet delight to walk on a narrow bank, near the sea; and have an itch to imitate these doubtful examples, wherein there is great danger of miscarrying.

SIXTH SORT.

Mixed examples; which contain in them a

double action, the one good, and the other bad, so closely couched together that it is a very hard thing to sever them. Thus, in the unjust steward, there was his wisdom to provide for himself, which God doth commend: and his wickedness, to purloin from his master, which God cannot but condemn. Thus, in the Hebrew midwives, (Exod. i.,) when they told the lie, there was in them *fides mentis, et fallacia mentientis,* the "faithfulness" of their love to their countrymen, and the "falseness of their lying" to Pharaoh.

USE OF THEM.

Behold, here is wisdom, and let the man that hath understanding discreetly divide betwixt the gold and the dross, the wheat and the chaff; what he is to follow and imitate, and what to shun and avoid. In the first year of the reign of Queen Elizabeth, the students of Christ-Church in Oxford buried the bones of Peter Martyr's wife in the same coffin with the ashes of Fridswick, a Popish saint; to this intent, that if Popery (which God forbid!) should ever after overspread this land, Papists should be puzzled to part the ashes of a supposed heretic from one of their canonized saints. Thus, in some actions of God's saints in the Bible, which are of a mixed nature; wickedness doth so insensibly unite and incorporate itself with that that is good, that it is very difficult to sever and divide them without a sound and well advised judgment.

ABUSE OF THEM.

In such as leave what is good, take what is bad; follow what is to be shunned, shun what is to be followed.

SEVENTH SORT.

Actions absolutely bad, so that no charitable comment can be fastened upon them, except we will incur the prophet's curse and woe, to "call good evil, and evil good." Such were the drunkenness of Noah, the incest of Lot, the lying of Abraham, the swearing of Joseph, the adultery of David, the denial of Peter.

USE OF THEM.

Let us read in them, first, a lecture of our own infirmity. Who dare warrant his armour for proof, when David's was shot through? Secondly, let us admire and laud God's mercy, who pardoned and restored these men on their unfeigned repentance. Lastly, let us not despair of pardon ourselves: if through infirmity overtaken, God in like manner is merciful to forgive us.

ABUSE OF THEM.

When men either make these their patterns, by which they sin; or, after their sinning, allege them for their excuse and defence. Thus Judith did. (Judith ix. 2.) For whereas that murder which Simeon and Levi did commit upon the Shechemites, (Gen. xxxiv. 25,) was cursed by Jacob, as a most heinous and horrible sin; yet she propounds it as a heroic act, and the unworthy precedent for her imitation: "O Lord God of my father Simeon, to whom thou gavest the sword to take vengeance on the strangers, which opened the womb of a maid, and defiled her," &c. Well, if the arm of Judith had been as weak as her judgment was herein, I should scarce believe that she ever cut off the head of Holophernes.

EIGHTH SORT.

Actions which are only good as they are qualified with such a circumstance, as David's eating the showbread in a case of absolute necessity; which otherwise was provided for the priests alone. Such are the doing of servile works on the Lord's Day, when in case of necessity they leave off to be *opera servilia,* and become *opera misericordiæ.*

USE OF THEM.

Let us be sure, in imitating of these, to have the same qualifying circumstance, without which otherwise the deed is impious and damnable.

ABUSE OF THEM.

In those which imitate the example without any heeding that they are so qualified as the action requires.

NINTH SORT.

The ninth and last sort remains; and such are

those which are eminently good; as, the faith of Abraham, the meekness of Moses, the valour of Joshua, the sincerity of Samuel, the plain dealing of Nathanael, &c. Follow not, then, the infidelity of Thomas, but the faith of Abraham; the testiness of Jonah, but the patience of Job; the adultery of David, but the chastity of Joseph: not the apostasy of Orpah, but the perseverance of Ruth here in my text.

AN ILL MATCH WELL BROKEN OFF.

1 JOHN II. 15:

Love not the world.

THE Stoics said to their affections, as Abimelech spake to Isaac, (Gen. xxvi. 16,) "Get you out from amongst us; for you are too strong for us." Because they were too strong for them to master, they therefore would have them totally banished out of their souls, and labour to becalm themselves with an apathy. But far be it from us, after their example, to root out such good herbs (instead of weeds) out of the garden of our nature; whereas affections, if well used, are excellent, if they mistake not their true object, nor exceed in their due measure. Joshua killed not the Gibeonites, but condemned them to be "hewers of wood and drawers of water for the sanctuary." We need not expel passions out of us, if we could conquer them, and make Grief draw water-buckets of tears for our sins, and Anger kindle fires of zeal and indignation when we see God dishonoured. But as that must needs be a deformed face, wherein there is a transposition of the colours,—the blueness of the vines being set in the lips; the redness which should be in the cheeks, in the nose,—so, alas! most misshapen is our soul, since Adam's fall, whereby our affections are so inverted, joy stands where grief should, grief in the place of joy. We are bold where we should fear, fear where we should be bold; love what we should hate, hate what we should love. This gave occasion to the blessed apostle, in my text, to dissuade men from loving that whereon too many dote. "Love not the world."

For the better understanding of which words, know that the devil goes about to make an unfitting match, betwixt the soul of a Christian, on the one party, and this world, on the other. A match too likely to go on, if we consider the simplicity and folly of many Christians, (because of the remnants of corruption,) easily to be seduced and inveigled, or the bewitching, enticing, alluring nature of this world: but God by St. John in my text forbiddeth the banns: "Love not the world."

In prosecuting whereof, we will first show the worthiness of a Christian soul; then we will consider the worthlessness of the world; and from the comparing of these two, this doctrine will result, that

It is utterly unfitting for a Christian to place his affections on worldly things.

Let us take notice of a Christian's possessions, and of his possibilities; what he hath in hand, and what he holdeth in hope. In possession he hath the favour of God; the Spirit of adoption crying in him, "Abba, Father;" and many excellent graces of sanctification in some measure in his heart. In hope and expectance he hath the reversion of heaven and happiness, (a reversion not to be got after another's death, but his own,) and those happinesses which eye cannot see, nor ear hear, neither it can enter into the heart of man to conceive.

Now see the worthlessness of the world. Three loadstones commonly attract men's affections, and make them to love,—beauty, wit, and wealth.

Beauty the world hath none at all. I dare boldly say, the world put on her holiday apparel, when she was presented by the devil to our Saviour. (Matt. iv. 9.) She never looked so smug and smooth before or since; and had there been any real beauty therein, the eagle sight of our Saviour would have seen it: yet, when all the glory of the world was proffered unto Him at the price of idolatry, He refused it. Yet, as old Jezebel, when she wanted true beauty, stopped up the leaks of age with adulterated complexion, and painted her face; so the world, in default of true beauty, decks herself with a false appearing fairness, which serves to allure amorous fools, and (to give the world, as well as the devil, her due) she hath for the time a kind of a pleasing fashionableness. But what saith St. Paul? Παράγει γὰρ τὸ σχῆμα τοῦ κόσμου τούτου, "The fashion of this world passeth away." (1 Cor. vii. 31.) The *wit* of the world is as little as her beauty, however it may be cried up by some of her fond admirers; yet as it is, 1 Cor. iii. 19, "The wisdom of this world is foolishness with God;" and *Cuilibet artifici credendum est in suâ arte;* what Wisdom itself counts foolishness is folly to purpose.

Her *wealth* is as small as either: what the world calls "substance" is most subject to accidents, uncertain, unconstant; even lands themselves in this respect are moveables. "Riches make themselves wings, and fly away;" they may leave us whilst we live; but we must leave them when we die.

Seeing, then, the world hath so little, and the Christian soul so much, let us learn a lesson of holy pride, to practise heavenly ambition. Descend not so far, O Christian, beneath thyself; remember what thou art, and what thou hast; lose not thyself in lavishing thy affections on so disproportioned a mate. There is a double disparity betwixt thy soul and the world.

First, that of *age*. Perchance the world might make a fit mate for thy old man, thy unregenerate half, thy relics of sin; but to match the old, rotten, withered, worm-eaten world to thy new man, thy new creature, the regenerated and renewed part of thy soul, grey to green, is rather a torture than a marriage,—altogether disproportionable.

Secondly, that of *quality or condition*. Thou art God's free-man. "If I have freed you," saith Christ, "then are you free indeed;" the world is, or ought to be, thy slave, thy vassal. "For whosoever is born of God overcometh the world: and this is the victory that overcometh the world, even our faith." (1 John v. 4.) Be not then so base as to make thy vassal thy mate. Alexander denied to marry Darius's daughter, though proffered unto him; scorning to be conquered by her beauty, whose father he had conquered by his valour. Let us not make the world our mistress, whereof we ought to be the master, nor prostitute our affections to a slave we have conquered.

OBJECTION.

Yea, may some say, this is good counsel, if it came in due season. Alas! now it cometh too late, after I have not only long doted, but am even wedded to this world. Infant affection may be easily crushed, but who can tame an old and rooted love? Think you that I have my affection in my hand, as hunters their dogs, to let slip or rate off at pleasure? How then shall I unlove the world, which hath been my bosom darling so long?

ANSWER.

Art thou wedded to the world? then instantly send her a bill of divorce. It need never trouble thy conscience; that match may be lawfully broken off, which was first most unlawfully made. Yea, thou wert long before contracted to God in thy baptism, wherein thou didst solemnly promise thou wouldst "forsake the devil and all his works; the vain pomp and glory of this world." Let the first contract stand; and because it is difficult for those who have long doted on the world to unlove her, we will give some rules, how it may be done by degrees. For indeed it is not to be done on a sudden; (matters of moment cannot be done in a moment;) but it is the task of a man's whole life, till the day of his death.

RULES HOW TO UNLOVE THE WORLD.

1. Look not with the eyes of covetousness or admiration on the things of the world. The eye is the principal Cinqueport of the soul, wherein love first arrives: *Ut vidi, ut perii!* Now thou mayest look on the things of the world, *ut in transitu*, "as in passage;" (otherwise we should be forced to shut our eyes;) and we may behold them with a slighting, neglectful, fastidious look. But

take heed to look * on them with a covetous eye, as Eve on the forbidden fruit, and Achan on the wedge of gold. Take heed to look * on them with the eye of admiration, as the disciples looked on the buildings of the temple, (Matt. xxiv. 1,) wondering at the eternity of the structure, and conceiving the arch of this world would fall as soon as such stones, riveted to immortality, might be dissolved. Wherefore our Saviour checketh them, "Verily I say unto you, There shall not be left one stone upon another, that shall not be cast down." Excellently Job, (xxxi. 1,) "I have made a covenant with mine eyes, that I should not behold a woman." A covenant? But what was the forfeiture Job's eyes were to pay in case he brake it? It is not expressed on the bond; but surely the penalty is implied,—many brackish tears, which his eyes in repentance must certainly pay, if they observed not the covenant.

2. Silence that spokesman in thy bosom; I mean, the allurements of the flesh and devil, who improveth his utmost power to advance a match betwixt thy soul and the world. And when any breach happens between thee and the world, so that thou art ready to cast her off, the flesh in thy bosom pleads her cause. "Why wilt thou," saith it, "deprive thyself of those contentments

* [*i. e.*, "against looking," as we should now express it.—ED.]

which the world would afford thee? Why dost thou torment thyself before thy time? Ruffle thyself in the silks of security; it will be time enough to put on the sackcloth of repentance, when thou liest on thy deathbed." Hearken not to the flesh, her enchantments; but as Pharaoh charged Moses to get him out of his presence, he should "see his face no more," (Exod. x. 28,) so strive, as much as in thee lieth, to expel these fleshly suggestions from thy presence, to banish them out of thy soul; at leastwise to silence them; though the mischief is, it will be muttering, and though it dare not halloo, it will still be whispering unto thee, in behalf of the world, its old friend, to make a reconciliation betwixt you.

3. Send back again to the world the love tokens she hath bestowed upon thee; I mean, those ill-gotten goods which thou hast gotten by indirect and unwarrantable means. As for those goods which thy parents left thee, friends have given thee, or thou hast procured by Heaven's providence on thy lawful endeavours, these are no love-tokens of the world, but God's gifts; keep them, use them, enjoy them, to His glory. But goods gotten by wrong and robbery, extortion and bribery, force and fraud, these restore and send back: for the world knoweth that she hath a kind of tie and engagement upon thee, so long as thou keepest her tokens; and in a manner thou art obliged in

honour, as long as thou detainest the gifts that were hers. Imitate Zaccheus: see how he casts back what the world gave him: "Behold, Lord, the half of my goods I give to the poor; and if I have taken any thing from any man by false accusation, I restore him fourfold." (Luke xix. 8.)

4. Set thy affections on the God of heaven. The best wedge to drive out an old love is to take in a new.

*Postquam nos Amaryllis habet, Galatea reliquit.**

Yea, God deserves our love first, because God "loved us first." (1 John iv. 19.) It is enough, indeed, to blunt the sharpest affection, to be returned with scorn and neglect; but it is enough to turn ice into ashes, to be first beloved by One that so well deserves love. Secondly, His is a lasting love: "Having loved His own that were in the world, He loved them to the end." (John xiii. 1.) Some men's affection spends itself with its violence, hot at hand, but cold at length; God's [is] not so, it is continuing. It is recorded in the honour of our King Henry the Seventh,† that he never discomposed favourite, one only excepted, which was William, Lord Stanley; a rare

* [Virgil, Ecl. i., 31.—ED.]
† Look [at] Lord Bacon in his Life.

matter, since many princes change their favourites, as well as their clothes, before they are old. But the observation is true of the Lord of Heaven without any exception : those who are once estated in His favour, He continues loving unto them to the end.

Hark, then, how He woos us, Isai. lv. 1 : "Ho, every one that thirsteth, come ye to the waters, and he that hath no money; come," &c. How He woos us, Matt. xi. 28 : "Come unto Me, all ye that labour and are heavy laden, and I will give you rest." Love His love-letter, His Word; His love-tokens, His sacraments; His spokesman, His ministers, which labour to favour the match betwixt Him and thy soul. But beware of two things.

1. Take heed of that dangerous conceit, that at the same time thou mayest keep both God and the world, and love these outward delights, as a concubine to thy soul. Nay, God He is "a jealous God;" He will have all, or none at all. There is a city in Germany, pertaining half to the bishop thereof, and half to the duke of Saxony, who named the city Myndyn, that is, "Mine and thine;" because it was theirs *communi jure*, and at this day by corruption it is called Minden.* But God will admit of no such divisions; He will hold nothing in coparceny; He will not share or-

* Munster's Cosmog., de Germ., lib. iii., p. 143.

part stakes with any; but He will have all entire to Himself alone.

2. Take heed thou dost not only fall out with the world, to fall in with it again, according to that,—

*Amantium iræ amoris redintegratio est.**

For even as some furious gamesters, when they have a bad game, throw their cards out of their hands, and vow to play no more; (not so much out of mislike of gaming as of their present game;) but when the cards run on their side, they are reconciled to them again; so many men, when the world frowns on them and crosses them, and they miss some preferment they desire, then a qualm of piety comes over their hearts; they are mortified on a sudden, and disavow to have any further dealing with worldly contentments. But when the world smiles on them again, favours and prospers them, they then return to their former love, and doting upon it. Thus Demas (2 Tim. iv. 10) would needs have another farewell embrace of the world, even after his solemn conversion to Christianity: " Demas hath forsaken me, having loved this present world." But when we are once at variance with the world, let us continue at deadly eternal feuds with it; and as it is said

* [Terence, *Andria*, iii., iii., 24.—ED.]

of Amnon, (2 Sam. xiii. 15,) that "the hatred wherewith he hated his sister Tamar was greater than the love wherewith he had loved her;" so, (what was cruelty in him will be Christianity in us,) once fallen out with the world, let the joint be never set again, that it may be the stronger; but let our hatred be immortal, and so much the stronger by how much our love was before.

GOOD FROM BAD FRIENDS.

2 SAM. XV. 31:

And one told David, saying, Ahithophel is among the conspirators with Absalom.

THIS text is a glass, wherein God's justice is plainly to be seen. David had formerly falsely forsaken Uriah, and now God suffers Ahithophel to forsake David.

Uriah neither in loyalty nor valour, though placed the last in the list, of the list of David's worthies, was any whit inferior to any of David's subjects. How did he sympathize with God's ark, and his fellow soldiers, stayed still in the camp, though he was in the king's court, in that he would not embrace those delights the marriage bed did afford him! No, though they practised upon him to make him drunk, yet in his drunkenness he was so sober, that all their wine washed not from him his first resolution, but he remained still constant. But how falsely did David forsake him, sending him with that snake in his bosom, which was to sting him to death! I mean the letter, which was Uriah's passport to his own grave. Well, Uriah placed much confidence in the love of David, who deceives him: David, with no less trust, relies on the loyalty of Ahithophel, and see what my text saith: "And one told David, saying, Ahithophel is also among the conspirators with Absalom."

OBSERVATION I.

Before we go farther, let us learn, *when our friends forsake us, to enter into a serious scrutiny of our own souls.* Hast thou never played foul or false with thy friend; if not in action, yet in intention? Dost thou not mean to prove base, if put to the trial, and if occasion be offered to deceive him? If so, know, thy false friend hath only got the start of thee, and played the foregame, doing what thou meanest to do. Rail not, then, on the times, nor speak satires against the faithlessness of men; but, laying thy hand on thy mouth, confess God hath justly found thee out, and dealt with thee as He did with David.

OBSERVATION II.

Secondly, hence we may observe, *the most politic heads have not always the faithfullest hearts.* Ahithophel was the Jewish Nestor, or their Solomon before Solomon, and like "the oracle of God for his wisdom," but like the oracle of the devil for his deceitfulness; for, whilst David swayed the sceptre, who more loyal to him than Ahithophel? and once when David is in banishment, he falls first to Absalom; he loved to worship the sun rising; yea, whilst David, the true sun, was but overcast with a cloud, he falls adoring that blazing star, that comet, only fed with the evaporations of pride and ambition, which shined for a while, and then went out in a stink.

REASONS WHY THE MOST POLITIC ARE NOT ALWAYS THE MOST FAITHFUL.

1. Because that cement which conglutinates hearts, and makes true friends indeed, is grace and goodness, whereof many politic heads are utterly devoid. 1 Cor. i. 26: "For ye see your calling, brethren, how that not many wise men after the flesh, not many mighty, not many noble, are called."

2. Politic men make their own profit the rule and square of their loves; they steer their course by the pole-star of their own good; and as in their actions, so in their affections, have an invisible end to themselves, which beginneth where that end endeth, which is apparent to others.

USE.

Do not, then, undervalue and despise the love of those who are of mean and inferior parts. Wise men have made use of such servants, and found them more manageable and more profitable; though their judgments were weaker, their affections might be stronger, than wiser men.

OBSERVATION III.

Thirdly, observe, *false friends will forsake thee in time of adversity*. He that believeth, that all those who smile on him and promise fair in time of prosperity, will perform it in time of his want, may as well believe, that all the leaves that be on trees at Midsummer will hang there as fresh and as fair on New Year's Day.

Come we now to consider, what good uses one may make to himself from the unfaithfulness of friends, when they forsake us.

1. First, consider with thyself, whether thou hast not been faulty in entertaining tale-bearers, and lending a listening ear unto them. Solomon saith, "A whisperer separateth chief friends." (Prov. xvi. 28.) Whithersoever he cometh, he bringeth with him the fire, fuel, and bellows of contention.

2. If herein thy conscience accuse thee not, examine thyself, whether there was not a *læsum principium* in the first initiation of your love. How came you acquainted? whereout grew your amity? whereon was your intimacy grounded? Didst thou not first purchase his favour with the price of a sin? For, know, friends unjustly gotten are not long comfortably enjoyed. Thus Absalom

by sordid flattery stole the hearts of the Israelites, descending too much beneath himself; (2 Sam. xv. 5;) as always ambitious spirits, when they would personate humility, over-act their part, and play baseness. We see king Hezekiah, who procured Sennacherib's love by his sacrilege, enjoyed not that purchase which he made God and His temple pay for. (2 Kings xviii. 16.) For Sennacherib no sooner received his money, but, *hoc non obstante*, [he] persisted in his former enmity and hostility against the Jews, and, as it followeth in the very next verse, sent up his captains to besiege Jerusalem.

3. If there be no fault in the inchoation, examine, hath there been none in the continuance of your friendship? Hast thou not committed many sins, to hold in with him? If so, then it is just with God He should forsake thee. Thus tyrants oftentimes cut off those stairs by which they climb up to their throne: yea, good princes have oftentimes justly sacrificed those their favourites to the fury of the people, who formerly have been the active instruments to oppress the people, though to the enriching of their princes. Hast thou not flattered him in his faults, or at leastwise by thy silence consented to him? If so, God hath now opened thy friend's eyes; he sees thy false dealing with him, and hath just cause to cast thee out of his favour.

When Amnon had defiled his sister Tamar, the text saith, (2 Sam. xiii. 15,) that "the hatred wherewith he hated her was greater than the love wherewith he had loved her." Poor lady! she was in no fault; not the cause, but only the object and the occasion, of her brother's sin; and that against her will, by his violence. Now, to reason *à minore ad majus*: if Amnon, in cold blood viewing the heinousness of his offence, so hated Tamar, which only concurred passively in his transgression, how may our friends justly hate us, if haply we have been the causers, movers, and procurers of their badness! If we have added fuel to the flame of their riot, played the panders to their lusts, and spurred them on in the full speed of their wantonness, deserve we not (when their eyes are opened, to see what foes we have been unto them, under pretended friendship) to be spit in the face, kicked out of their company, and to be used with all contumely and disgrace?

4. Hast thou not idolatrized to thy friend? Hath he not totally monopolized thy soul, so that thou hast solely depended on him, without looking higher or further? *Tu patronus; si deseris tu, perimus.* Thus too many wives anchor all their hopes for outward matters on their husbands, and too many children lean all their weight on their fathers' shoulders; so that it is just with God to suffer these their wooden pillars to break, on whom they lay too much heft.

5. Hast thou not undervalued thy friend, and set too mean a rate and low an estimate on his love? If so, God hath now taught thee the worth of a pearl by losing it. And this comes often to pass, though not in our friends' voluntary deserting us, as Ahithophel did David, yet in their leaving us against their wills, when God taketh them from us by death.

QUESTION.

But there this question may be demanded: Whether is one ever again to receive him for his friend, and to restore him to the old state of his favour, who once hath deceived and dealt falsely with him?

ANSWER.

Many circumstances are herein well to be weighed. First, did he forsake thee out of frailty and infirmity, or out of mere spite and maliciousness? Secondly, hath he since showed any tokens and evidences of unfeigned sorrow? Hath he humbled himself unto thee, and begged God's and thy pardon? If he hath offended mischievously, and persists in it obstinately, O let not the strength of thy supposed charity so betray thy judgment as to place confidence in him! Samson was blind, before he was blind; the lust of Delilah deprived him of his eyes, before the Philistines bored them out, in that, once and again being deceived by Delilah, he still relied on her word.

But if he hath showed himself such a penitent, and thou art verily persuaded of his repentance, receive him again into thy favour. Thus dealt our Saviour with St. Peter, Mark xvi. 7 : " But go your way, tell His disciples and Peter,"—Peter especially; Peter that had sinned, and Peter that had sorrowed; Peter that had denied his Master, but Peter that "went out and wept bitterly."

6. Sixthly, and lastly, it may be God suffers thy friends to prove unfaithful to thee, to make thee stick more closely to Himself. Excellent to this purpose is that place, Micah vii. 5 : " Trust ye not in a friend, put ye no confidence in a guide : keep the doors of thy mouth from her that lieth in thy bosom. *For* the son dishonoureth the father, the daughter riseth up against the mother, the daughter-in-law against her mother-in-law; a man's enemies are the men of his own house." But now mark what follows : " Therefore will I look unto the Lord ; I will wait for the God of my salvation." As if he had said, " Is the world at this bad hand,—is it come to this bad pass,—that one must be far from trusting their nearest friends ? It is well, then, I have one fast Friend, on whom I may rely, the God of heaven." I must confess, these words of the prophet are principally meant of the time of persecution, and so are applied by our Saviour, Matt. x. 21. However, they contain an eternal truth, whereof good use may be made

at any time. Let us therefore, when our friends forsake us, principally rely on God, who hath these two excellent properties of a friend: first, He is near to us: so saith the Psalmist, "Thy name is near, and this do Thy excellent works declare." They have a speedy way of conveying letters from Aleppo to Babylon, sending them by a winged messenger, tied to the legs of a dove: but we have a shorter cut to send our prayers to God, by sending our prayers by the wings of the Holy Spirit, that heavenly Dove, whereby they instantly arrive in heaven. As God is near to us, so He is ever willing and able to help us. On Him, therefore, let us ever rely; and when other reeds bow or break, or run into our hands, let us make Him to be our staff, whereon we may lean ourselves.

A GLASS FOR GLUTTONS.

ROMANS XIII. 13:

Not in gluttony.

THESE words are a parcel of that Scripture that converted St. Augustine. He (as he confesseth of himself) at the first was both erroneous in his tenets, and vicious in his life; when, running on in full career in wickedness, God stopped him with His voice from heaven, *Tolle et lege,* "Take up thy book, and read;" and the first place which God directed his eye to was these words in my text; and after this time, being reclaimed, he proved a worthy instrument of God's glory, and the church's good. Now as those receipts in physic are best, which are confirmed under the broad seal of experience, and set forth with the privilege of *Probatum est;* so my text may challenge a priority before other places of Scripture, because upon record it hath been the occasion to convert so famous a Christian. Neither think that the virtue of these words are extracted by doing of this one cure, or that my text, with Isaac, hath only one blessing for him that came first; no, by God's blessing it may be cordial for the saving of our souls. To-day, therefore, part of Samson's riddle shall be fulfilled in your ears: "Out of the devourer came meat." Gluttony, that vice which consumeth and devoureth food,— the discourse thereof by God's assistance shall feed us at this time.

Not in gluttony.

DOCTRINE.

Gluttony is a dangerous sin for any Christian to be guilty of.

REASON.

Because human laws have provided no penalty for it. Men will be afraid to commit petty larceny, for fear of whipping; felony, for fear of branding; murder, for fear of hanging; worse sins, for fear of having a grave, whilst living. But it is too likely that men will take leave and liberty to themselves to be gluttons, presuming upon hope of impunity, because man's laws have ordered no punishment for it. Yet as those offences are accounted the greatest which cannot be punished by a constable, a justice, or judge of assize, but are reserved immediately to be punished by the king himself; so gluttons must needs be sinners in a high degree, who are not censurable by any earthly king, but are referred to be judged at God's tribunal alone.

REASON II.

Because it is so hard and difficult to discern. Like to the hectic fever, it steals on a man unawares. Some sins come with observation, and are either ushered with a noise, or, like a snail, leave a slime behind them, whereby they may be traced and tracked, as drunkenness. The Ephraimites were differenced from the rest of the Israelites by their lisping; they could not pronounce *H*, which then was a heavy aspiration unto them, when it cost the lives of so many thousands. Thus drunkards are distinguished from the king's sober subjects by clipping the coin of the tongue. But there are not such signs and symptoms of gluttony. This sin doth so insensibly unite and incorporate itself with our natural appetite, to eat for the preservation of our lives, that, as St. Gregory saith,* "it is a hard thing to discern," *quid necessitas petat, et quid voluptas suppetat, quia per esum voluptas necessitati miretur,*—what is the full charge of food which nature requires for our sustenance, and what is that sure charge which is heaped by superfluity.

REASON III.

Because of the sundry dangers it brings. First, to the soul. Luke xxi. 34: "Take heed lest your

---

* *Moral.*, lib. xxx., cap. 28, *ante medium.*

hearts be oppressed with surfeiting." And indeed the soul must needs be unfitting to serve God, being so encumbered. That man hath but an uncomfortable life, who is confined to live in a smoky house. The brain is one of these places of the residence of the soul; and when that is filled with steams and vapours arising from unconcocted crudities in the stomach, the soul must needs *malè habitare*, " dwell uncheerfully," ill accommodated in so smoky a mansion. And as hereby it is unapt for the performance of good, so it is ready for most evil, for uncleanness, scurrility, ill-speaking; this being the reason, saith St. Gregory, why Dives's tongue was so tormented in hell, because he, being a glutton, with his tongue had most dishonoured God.

Secondly, this sin impairs the health of the body. The outlandish proverb saith, that " the glutton digs his grave with his own teeth,"— hastens his death by his intemperance. For, if there were a conflict in Rebekah's body, when two twins were in her womb, must there not be a battle and insurrection in his stomach, wherein there is meat, hot, cold, sod, roast, flesh, fish? And which side soever wins, nature and health will be overcome, whenas a man's body is like unto the ark of Noah, containing all beasts, clean and unclean; but he the most unclean beast, that contains them. Our law interprets it to be murder, when one is killed with a knife. Let us take heed we be not all condemned by God for being felons *de se;* for wilful murdering our own lives with our knives by our superstitious * eating.

Thirdly, it wrongs the creatures that hereby are abused. Indeed, they willingly serve man, so long as he is a king over them; but they are loath to do it, when he turns tyrant: so if when the drunkard sings, the drink sighs; when the glutton laughs, the meat grieves to be so vainly misspent by him. God saith, (Hosea ii. 9,) that He will recover His flax and His wool from the idolatrous Jews; *Vindicabo,* "I will rescue and recover them," as from slavery and subjection, wherein they were detained against their will. And in such like tyranny are the creatures, as bread, wine, and meat, tortured under the glutton.

Lastly, it wrongeth the poor; for it is the overmuch feasting of Dives which of necessity maketh the fasting of Lazarus; and might not the superfluous meat of the rich be sold for many a pound, and given to the poor?

Come we now to consider, wherein gluttony doth consist. I am not ignorant of that verse in Thomas [Aquinas]:

Præproperè, lautè, nimis, ardenter, studiosè:

but I will not march in Saul's heavy armour, or

* [Perhaps a misprint for *superfluous.*—ED.]

confine myself to follow the schools' directions herein. I will go against this Goliath of gluttony with my own sling and stone, and use a private and plain method. This sin, therefore, consisteth either in the quantity of the meat, or in the quality, or in the manner of eating.

1. In the quantity. And here it is hard to define the omer of manna for every man's belly; the proportion of meat for every man's stomach. That quantity of rain will make a clay ground drunk, which will scarce quench the thirst of a sandy country. It is thus also in men; that proportion of meat surfeiteth and surchargeth the stomachs of some, which is not enough to satisfy the hunger of others, especially of those who, being young, have hot and quick digestion; of those who, living in a cold climate, thereby have the heat of their stomachs intended;* of those whose stomachs are strong, by reason of their labour and travail. And not to speak of the disease called *boulimia*,—men's natures being thus diverse, by what standard shall I measure them? Let this be the rule: he shall be arraigned and condemned before God for gluttony in the quantity of meat, who hath eaten so much as thereby he is disabled, either in part, or wholly, to serve God in his general or particular calling, be his age, climate, or temper whatsoever.

* [*i. e.*, intensified.—ED.]

2. In quality; and that four ways. (1.) When the meat is too young. Exodus xxiii. 19 : " Thou shalt not seethe a kid in his mother's milk;" that is, Thou shalt not eat it before it hath age to be just and firm flesh. Circumcision was deferred till the eighth day; one reason rendered by divines is, because a child before that time is not *caro consolidata;* and sure there is a time, before which beasts and fowls are not solid, fast, and lawful to be eaten. I must confess, we are to live by the creatures' death; they, being born, are condemned to die, for our necessity or pleasure; and these condemned persons desire not a pardon, but deserve a reprieve, that they may be respited and reserved so long, till they be good and wholesome food, and not clapt into the glutton's bowels, before they be scarce out of their mother's belly.

(2.) Secondly, when the meat is too costly. Thus Cleopatra macerated an union, a pearl of an inestimable worth, and drank it in a health to Mark Anthony; a deed of hers as vain as the other wicked, when she poisoned herself.

(3.) Thirdly, when the meats are only incentives and provocations to lusts, in some kind thereof. I could instance, were I not afraid to teach sin by confuting it. Why is the furnace made seven times hotter than ever it was before? Is not the devil of himself sufficiently mischievous? Is not our own corruption of itself sufficiently forward, yea, headlong to evil, but also we must advantage them by our own folly? Have we vowed in our baptism to fight against, and do we ourselves send armour and munition to, our enemy? Yea, many set their own houses on fire, and then complain they burn.

*Labor est inhibere volantes :
Parce, puer, stimulis, et fortiùs utere loris.* *

(4.) Lastly, when the meat is such as is only to increase appetite; when one before is plentifully fed. Such is the cruelty of the Spanish Inquisition, that when they have brought a man to the door of death, they will not let him go in; when by exquisite tortures they have almost killed him, then by comfortable cordials they do again revive him; and whereas of God "it is appointed for all men once to die," these men's cruelty makes men to die often. Thus men, when they have stabbed and killed hunger with plentiful eating, with sauce and salt meats of purpose they restore it again to life; and for several times, according to their own pleasures, kill and recall, stab and revive their appetites.

3. In the manner of eating.
(1.) Greedily, without giving thanks to God;

* [Ovid, *Metamorph.*, ii. 128, 127.—Ed.]

like hogs, eating up the mast, not looking up to the hand that shaketh it down. It is said of the Israelites, (Exod. xxxii. 6,) " The people sat down to eat and to drink,"—there is no mention of grace before meat,—" and rose up to play,"— there is no mention of grace after.

(2.) Secondly, constantly. Dives fared deliciously every day; there was no Friday in his week, nor fast in his almanack, nor Lent in his year: whereas the moon is not always in the full, but hath as well a waning as a waxing; the sea is not always in a spring-tide, but hath as well an ebbing as a flowing. And surely the very rule of health will dictate thus much to a man, not always to hold a constant tenure of feasting, but sometimes to abate in their diets.

(3.) Lastly, when they eat their meats studiously, revolving all the powers of their mind upon meat, singing Requiems in their soul, with the glutton in the Gospel, "Soul, take thine ease," &c. And whereas we are to eat to live, these only live to eat.

Let us therefore beware of the sin of gluttony; and that for these motives.

MOTIVE I.

Because it is the sin of England; for though, without usurpation, we may entitle ourselves to the pride of the Spanish, jealousy of the Italian, wantonness of the French, drunkenness of the

A GLASS FOR GLUTTONS. 155

Dutch, and laziness of the Irish; and though these outlandish sins have of late been naturalized and made free denizens of England; yet our ancientest carte is for the sin of gluttony.

MOTIVE II.

It is the sin of our age. Our Saviour saith, (Matt. xxiv. 37,) "But as it was in the days of Noah, so likewise shall the coming of the Son of Man be. They did eat and drink," &c. That is, excessively; for otherwise they did eat in all ages. It is said of old men that they are twice children: the same is true of this old doting world; it doth now revert and relapse into the same sins whereof it was guilty in the infancy: we, on whom the ends of the world are come, are given to the sins of gluttony, as in the days of Noah.

MOTIVE III.

The third motive is from the time. "These seven full ears, these seven fat kine," these seven weeks of feasting between Christmas and Shrovetide, are past; these seven lean ears, these seven lean kine, the seven fasting weeks in Lent, are now begun. Practise therefore the counsel which Solomon gives, Proverbs xxiii. 1: "When thou sittest to eat with a ruler, consider diligently what is before thee: and put thy knife to thy throat, if thou beest a man given to thy appetite." This is thy throat, that narrow passage of importance; guard it with thy knife, as with a halbert, that no superfluous meat pass that way, to betray thy soul to gluttony. But it is to be feared that we will rather turn the backs of our knives than the edges: I mean, we will use little violence to repress and restrain our own greediness. That our knives may therefore be the sharper, let these whetstones set an edge on them.

1. Consider, the bread that thou eatest is the bread that perisheth: and our Saviour saith, "Labour not for the meat that perisheth, but for that which endureth to everlasting life." Biscuit is but perishing bread, though it may last two years; for what is two years to eternity?

2. We shall perish that eat the meat, but God shall destroy both it and that. And then the glutton which hath played the epicure on meat whilst he lived, the worms shall play the epicures on him when he is dead; and whilst the temperate man shall give them but ordinary commons, the larded glutton shall afford them plentiful exceedings.

To conclude this point: wary was the practice of Job, (Job i. 5,) who, after the days of his sons' "feasting were gone about, offered burnt offerings" to God for them: for he said, "It may be my sons have sinned, and cursed God in their hearts."

So, sith [since] gluttony is so subtle a sin, and so hard to be discerned; when we have been at a great feast in the day, let us sacrifice our prayers to God, and sue out a pardon from Him, lest peradventure, in the heart of our mirth, without our knowledge, and against our will, we have inseverably been overtaken with the sin of gluttony.

HOW FAR GRACE CAN BE ENTAILED.

2 TIMOTHY I. 5:

When I call to remembrance the unfeigned faith which is in thee, which dwelt first in thy grandmother Lois, and thy mother Eunice; and I am persuaded that it is in thee also.

When I call to remembrance.

OBSERVATION I.

It is good to feed our souls on the memories of pious persons: partly that we may be moved to praise God in and for His graces, given to His saints; and partly that we may be incited to imitate the virtues of the deceased. Ahaz was so taken with the altar at Damascus, (2 Kings xvi. 10,) that he would needs have one at Jerusalem, made according to all the workmanship thereof. When we call to mind the virtues of the deceased, and cannot but be delighted with their goodness, let us labour to fashion ourselves after their frame, and to erect the like virtues in our own souls.

OBSERVATION II.

Godly children occasion their parents to be called to memory. St. Paul, beholding Timothy's goodness, is minded thereby to remember his mother and grandmother, Eunice and Lois: they can never be dead, whiles he is alive. Good children are the most lasting monument, to perpetuate their parents, and make them survive after death. Dost thou desire to have thy memory continued? Art thou ambitious to be revenged of Death, and to outlast her spite? It matters not for building great houses, and calling them after thy name; give thy children godly education, and the sight of their goodness will furbish up thy memory in the mouths and minds of others, that it never rusts in oblivion.

Which dwelt first.

That is, which was an inhabitant in their hearts. Faith in temporary believers is as a guest,—comes for a night, and is gone; at the best is but as a sojourner, lodges there for a time: but it *dwelleth*, maketh her constant residence and abode, in the saints and servants of God.

Grandmother Lois, and mother Eunice.

QUESTION.

Why doth not St. Paul mention the father of Timothy, but as it were blanch him over with silence?

ANSWER.

1. First, it is probable that St. Paul had not any special notice of him, or that he was dead before the apostle's acquaintance in that family.

2. Likely it is, he was not so eminent and appearing in piety. The weaker vessel may sometimes be a stronger vessel of honour. Yea, the text intimateth as much, Acts xvi. 1: "Behold, a certain disciple was there, named Timotheus, the son of a certain woman, which was a Jewess, and believed; but his father was a Greek." Let women labour in a holy emulation, to excel their husbands in goodness: it is no trespass of their modesty, nor breach of the obedience they vowed to their husbands in marriage, to strive to be superiors and above them in piety.

3. Eunice and Lois, the mother and grandmother, are only particularly mentioned, because deserving most commendation for instructing Timothy in his youth; as it is in chapter iii., verses 14, 15: "Knowing of whom thou hast learned them; and that from a child thou hast

known the Holy Scriptures." For the same reason the names of the mothers of the kings of Judah are so precisely recorded for their credit or disgrace, according to the goodness or badness of their sons. Let mothers drop instruction into their children with their milk, and teach them to pray when they begin to prattle.

DOCTRINE.

Though grace be not entailed from parent to child, yet the children of godly parents have a great advantage to religion; yea, that fivefold.

1. The advantage of the promise; yea, though they come but of the half blood, (much more if true born on both sides,)—if one of their parents be godly. "For the unbelieving husband is sanctified by the" believing "wife; and the unbelieving wife is sanctified by the husband: else were your children unclean; but now they are holy." (1 Cor. vii. 14.)

2. Of good precepts, some taught them in their infancy; so that they can easier remember what they learned than *when* they learned it. Genesis xviii. 19: "For I know Abraham, that he will command his children and his household after him to fear the Lord."

3. Of good precedents. *Habent domi unde discant:* whereas the children of evil parents see daily what they ought to shun and avoid, these behold what they should follow and imitate.

4. Of correction; which, though untoothsome to the palate to taste, is not unwholesome to the stomach to digest.

5. Of many a good prayer, and some no doubt steeped in tears, made for them before some of them were made. *Filius tantarum lacrymarum non peribit*, said St. Ambrose to Monica, of St. Augustine, her son.

Disdain thou, then, out of a holy pride, to be the vicious son to a virtuous father; to be the profane daughter of a pious mother: but labour to succeed as well to the lives as to the livings, the goodness as the goods, of thy parents.

OBJECTION.

"Yea, but," may the children of bad parents say, "this is but cold comfort for us;" and they may take up the words of the soldiers, Luke iii. 14: "And what shall we do?"

ANSWER I.

First, if thy parents be living, conceive not that their badness dispenseth with thy duty unto them. Thou hast the same cause—though not the same comfort—with good children to obey thy parents. This do labour, to gain them with thy conversation. It was incest and a foul sin in Lot to be husband to his daughters, and beget children on them; but it would be no spiritual incest in thee to be father to thy father, to beget him in grace who begat thee in nature; and, by the piety and amiableness of thy carriage, to be the occasion, by God's blessing, of his regeneration. And what Samuel said to the people of Israel, (1 Sam. xii. 23,) " God forbid that I should sin against the Lord in ceasing to pray for you;" so God forbid thou shouldest ever leave off to have thy knees bended, and thy hands lifted up, for the conversion of thy bad father.

Moreover, labour more especially to shun and avoid those sins to which thy father was addicted; and chiefly such sins, the inclination whereto may depend from the temper and constitution of the body; so that a proneness thereto may in some sort seem to be entailed to posterity. Was thy father notorious for wantonness? strive then to be noted for chastity. Was he infamous for pride? labour thou to be famous for humility. And though thou must not be dejected with grief at the consideration of the badness of thy parents, yet mayest thou make a sovereign use thereof, to be a just cause of humiliation to thyself.

If thy parents be dead, and if thou canst speak little good of them, speak little of them. What sullenness did in Absalom,—He "spake to his brother Amnon neither good nor bad," (2 Sam. xiii. 22,)—let discretion do in thee; seal up thy lips in silence; say nothing of thy parents. He is either a fool or a madman, who, being in much company, and not being urged thereunto, by any occasion will tell others, "My father lies in the Fleet;" "My father lies in prison, in the Counter." More witless is he who will speak both words uncharitable and unnatural concerning the final estate of his father, in an eternal bad condition.

And I am persuaded, there is a threefold kind of persuasion, whereby one may be persuaded of good in another man.

1. The persuasion of infallibility. And this only God hath. Acts xv. 18 : "Known unto God are all His works from the beginning of the world." He alone "searcheth and trieth the hearts and reins." And they also have it to whom God immediately reveals it. Thus Ananias knew that Paul was a true servant of God, after it was revealed to him: "For he is a chosen vessel unto Me, to bear My name before the Gentiles, and kings, and the children of Israel." (Acts ix. 15.) And in this sense of infallible persuasion we may understand St. Paul in the text; because it is said, 1 Tim. i. 18, "This commandment write I unto thee, son Timotheus, according to the prophecies which went before upon thee, that thou by them shouldst fight a good fight."

2. The persuasion of charity. And this, I must confess, is but weak, and rather a presumption than a persuasion. Charity "thinketh no evil;"

it "believeth all things, hopeth all things;" (1 Cor. xiii. 5, 7;) and in this kind of persuasion we conceive that all men have faith dwelling in them, of whom we know no just reason to conceive the contrary.

3. The persuasion of a well and strong grounded opinion; to make which, these three things must concur. First, the party that conceives this opinion must have a good judgment and discerning spirit, well to dive and pierce into the natures and dispositions of men. Secondly, he must be long acquainted with that person, of whom he hath such an opinion, that faith dwelleth in him. Too bold are these men who, upon a superficial knowledge and short conversing with any, dare peremptorily pronounce, that such an one hath saving grace and sanctity in him. These are professors of spiritual palmistry, who think that upon small experience they can see the "lifeline," the line of eternal life, in the hands of men's souls; whereas, for all their skill, they often mistake the hands of Esau for the hands of Jacob. Lastly, they must have intimate familiarity with them, and be not only their acquaintance [at] large, but in ordinary. *Te intus et in cute novi.** Put all these three together,—that one hath a discerning spirit, long and intimate acquaintance with one; and he may arrive at St.

* [Persius, Sat. iii., 30.—ED.]

Paul's persuasion in my text, to be persuaded of faith dwelling in him, with whom he hath been thus long and intimately acquainted. And in this sense (though it may be of the infallible persuasion by revelation) understand we that, 2 Kings iv. 1: "Now there cried a certain woman of the wives of the sons of the prophets unto Elisha, saying, Thy servant my husband is dead; and thou knowest that thy servant did fear the Lord."

Yet for all this we may set this down for a true position, that the wisest of men easily may [be], and sometimes are, deceived, in counting them good which are very counterfeits; and especially in these cases:—

1. First, in close-natured men, such as lie in at a close guard, and offer no play; whose well is deep, and men generally want buckets to measure them; so that one may live twenty years with them, and be never a whit the wiser, in knowing their disposition.

2. In various and inconstant men, which, like Proteus, never appear twice in the same shape, but differ as much from themselves as from other men, and are only certain in uncertainty; so that one can build no certain conclusion on such floating, flitting sands; and even know not what to make of them.

3. In men of an excellent nature, such as Titus

Vespasian, [who] was called *deliciæ humani generis*. This *euphuia* presents itself in all outward signs and symptoms; so like to grace that it is often mistaken for it. Whereas, on the other side, men of a rugged, unbrushed nature, such as were never licked, hewn, or polished, may be slandered in many men's judgments, to be altogether devoid of piety.

4. In affected dissemblers, hypocrisy is as like piety as hemlock to parsley; and many one hath been deceived therein.

To conclude: if we desire to pass a rational judgment on faith in others, and piety in their hearts, let us first labour to have true sanctity in our own. One complained to a philosopher, that it was a hard thing to find a wise man. "It is true," said he; "for he must first be a wise man that seeks him, and knows when he hath found him: so that, on the matter, it is not one wise man, but two wise men, must meet together." So it is a hard thing to know true sanctity in another man; because he must have true piety in himself that knows it, or else he is an incompetent judge to pass a verdict on another. Let us therefore labour first to have true grace in our hearts, that so, with St. Paul, we may be persuaded of grace that dwells in another.

A CHRISTENING SERMON.

2 KINGS V. 14:

Then went he down, and dipped himself seven times in Jordan, according to the saying of the man of God: and his flesh came again like to the flesh of a little child, and he was clean.

IN this chapter, Naaman the Syrian comes hurrying with his horses, and rattling with his chariot, to the door of the prophet Elisha, to be cured of his leprosy. Now he said in his heart, (I could not have told his thoughts, except first he had told them me,) "He will surely come out to me, and stand, and call on the name of the Lord his God, and strike his hand over the place, and recover the leper." Thus he thought, that the very noise of the wheels of his chariot should call Elisha to come to him. Because he was captain of the host of Syria, he thought to be commander of God's prophet; and he expected a great deal of service from him. And truly he might expect it: for the prophet beat him at his own weapon, out-shot him in his own bow, out-stated him in stateliness itself.

1. Called him not in, but let him stand at door.
2. Came not to him in his person, but by a proxy.
3. Sent him a plain and cold answer: "Wash seven times in Jordan."

By the way, I dare boldly say, Elisha in himself was not proud at other times. He could fare hardly on barley loaves, and feed hungerly on plain pottage; but at this time his affecting of state was both lawful and necessary.

First, it was the sight of Naaman's shoe, which made Elisha so high in the instep: with the stately, he would be stately; the rather because he did perceive that Naaman must be humbled before he could be healed, and the proud flesh first taken out of his heart ere the putrid flesh could be cured in his body.

Secondly, Naaman, though he was a prince, yet he was but a pagan; and in this respect the lowest Hebrew was higher than he. Elisha therefore would teach him to learn himself; that he was not proper to receive so great favours, as being but a goat, and no lost sheep of the fold of Israel.

Lastly, Elisha was an extraordinary man. He might well stand upon terms of double distance, who had a double portion of Elijah's spirit.

You my brethren of the ministry, let us know, that we succeed to the office, but not to the eminencies, to the place, but not to the personal perfections, of the prophet Elisha. And let us know, that humility is our honour and crown; so that except we be forced unto it against our wills, *se defendendo*, to maintain the honour of God and our office, to stand upon our points, let us, leaving the pattern of Elisha's stateliness, rather follow the precedent of St. Paul's humility: "I was made all things to all men, that by all means I might gain some."

To return to Naaman. The mention of the water put him into a fire; he burneth with choler and passion: " Are not Abana and Pharpar, rivers of Damascus, better than all the waters of Israel? May I not wash in them, and be clean? So he turned and went away in a rage." Well, his servants come to him, to persuade him, and bring with them good logic and ethics, good arguments and good manners. Good logic, reasoning *à minori ad majus*: " If the prophet had bid thee do some great thing, wouldest thou have not done it? How much rather then, when he saith to thee, Wash, and be clean?" Good ethics: " My father." " My "—all speaking in one person, so unanimously they consented in one opinion. " Father "—as if they had said, " We confess thou art wiser than we are, of more age, of more honour; yet you are near unto us, you are dear unto us, we wish your weal and welfare." O what a deal did they speak in a little, and how many sentences are comprised in this one word, "Father!" These words so wrought on Naaman that the lion became a lamb; he that formerly had conquered his foes, now subdues himself; down came he in his stomach, and down comes he in his person.

Then went he down, &c.

These words contain a cure most strange, most true; wherein observe,

1. The time wherein it was wrought: "Then."
2. The sick man, or—if you please, since his servants have persuaded him—the patient.
3. The disease: leprosy.
4. The physician: the man of God, Elisha.
5. The physic: $\begin{cases} quid, \text{ washing in Jordan;} \\ quoties, \text{ seven times.} \end{cases}$
6. The effect and operation thereof: "And his flesh came again like the flesh of a little child, and he was clean."

But as Gideon had too great an army for his use, and therefore sent most of his soldiers away; so the time commands me to dismiss most of these points, and only to retain such with me as are most pertinent to the present occasion.

I begin with the time wherein the cure was wrought: *Then.*

"Then." When? After his servants had persuaded him: whence observe,

OBSERVATION.

Wise men must sometimes follow the counsel of their inferiors, as Naaman did of his servants. The reason is, that wise men may be deceived in those actions wherein they themselves are parties and interested. It is possible that passion, prejudice, and partiality, one or all of these, like so many pearls, may blind the eyes of your judgment. Whereas such as look on may see more than those that play the game; and though in other respects their judgment be far inferior, yet herein they may be more clear, because less engaged. Yea, Solomon himself, though the wisest of kings, had a council of aged men, that stood before him. And though this might seem but the lighting of so many candles to the sun, yet no doubt he knew wisely to make use of them, who in wisdom were far beneath him. I have seen a dull whetstone set an edge on a knife: yea, the wisest of men need not think scorn to learn of the worst of men, when we may be taught not to take carking care by the lilies, and yet providently to provide from the pismire.

But then especially are we to listen to the counsel of inferiors, whose advice we know proceeds from a loving heart, and is aimed and levelled at our good; especially if they be such that our credit and profit is embarked in the same bottom with theirs; together they sink, and together they swim; so that we cannot suspect, dare not deny, and must confess, that their advice looks straight forward at our good, and squints not aside at any sinister respect. Wherefore, sometimes let Abraham hearken to Sarah his wife; Moses the Jew, to Jethro the Gentile; David the sovereign, to Joab the subject: yea, let not Apollos, though eloquent, and mighty in Scripture, think scorn to learn his Christ-cross from Aquila and Priscilla.

Yet when inferiors presume to commend their counsel to their superiors, let it be qualified with these cautions.

1. Let them do it seasonably, in a fit opportunity. Now opportunity is the spirits of time extracted, or the quintessence of time at large, distilled; and such an opportunity must he wait for, who hopes to do any good by his advice to his betters. Abigail was excellent hereat: she told her husband Nabal "nothing, less or more, until the morning light;" (1 Sam. xxv. 36;) either because she would not cast the pearl of her good counsel before a swine, wallowing in drunkenness; or because she thought her physic would work the better with him, if she gave it him fasting.

2. It must be done secretly. An open reproof of our betters is little better than a libel. True it

is, we ministers may publicly, when occasion is offered us, reprove the vices of those who in outward respects are far our superiors; yet we must do it publicly, secretly; publicly for the place, secretly for the manner. We are not to make in the pulpit such a hue and cry after the offender, that the capacity of the meanest may take him on suspicion, whom we mean. No, let us deliver our doctrine in common, and let the guilty conscience enclose it to itself.

3. They must do it with all reverence and humility, as the servants of Naaman in my text. A wool-pack doth conquer the strength of an ordnance, by yielding unto it: so there be many natures which will be led, but may not be drawn or dragged; and these may be broken with fair usage, that cannot be bowed with forcible dealing.

4. Let them pray to Him who hath the hearts of all men in His hand,—like the rivers of water, He turneth them whither He pleaseth,—that He would be pleased to prepare and mollify their hearts, to whom they are to address their counsel; that He would bow their ears to hear, their heads to conceive, and their hearts to practise, that advice which shall be commended to them for their good.

And so much for the time. Come we next, in the second place, to the physic prescribed,—water of Jordan. Whence observe,

OBSERVATION.

God appoints weak means, by the virtue of His institution, to accomplish great matters. Take a survey of all the parts of God's service, and we shall find this true. Begin at the font: there is plain water of Jordan; yet, by the virtue of God's ordinance, it washeth away original sin. Pass from the font to the minister's pew: there is still plain water of Jordan,—the weakness of the word, and the folly of preaching; yet God's wisdom and power, to make the goat a sheep, the lion a lamb, the wanton chaste, the passionate patient; yea, to revive such as are dead in trespasses and sins. Look on the minister: here is still plain water of Jordan,—earthen vessels, men loaden with infirmities, like the rest of their brethren; yet are they dispensers of the mysteries of God. Proceed to the communion table: there is still plain water of Jordan,—a morsel of bread, and a draught of wine; yet these, worthily received, sign and seal unto us the body of Christ, and the benefits of His passion.

USE.

Let us take heed that we take not exception at the simplicity of God's ordinance. A Spanish Don, having heard much of the fame of Calvin, travelled to Geneva, to see him; where finding him both plain in person and poor in apparel, he repented himself of his pains, and whom his ear did admire at distance, his eye did contemn when present. Just such valuers are carnal men of God's ordinances: they guess the jewel by the case, and think nothing can be good which is not gaudy. But surely, were our eyes anointed with that "eye-salve," mentioned Revelation iii. 18, then (as heralds account the plainest coats the most ancient, better than those of a later edition, which are so full of filling that they are empty of honour) we should see the inward state in the outward simplicity, and inward majesty in the outward meanness, of God's ordinance. When one of his courtiers showed the Great Turk the sword of Scanderbeg, "I see," said he, "no such miracles in this sword, rather than in any other, that it should achieve such victories." "Yea, but," said one that stood by, "if you had seen also Scanderbeg's arm, with what a mighty force he wielded this sword, you then would change your resolution." So, many say, they can see nothing in the water of baptism, more than in ordinary well water; they can see nothing in the world in the bread and wine in the Communion, [more] than in that in the baker's panniers or vintner's cellar; no more in a sermon than in a civil oration in a Guildhall of the same length. But if they saw the arm of God, with what a mighty strength He enforceth these ordinances, and how His invisible grace attendeth them, they would be of another mind. Gaze, then, no longer on Ehud's hand, for that was lame; or on his dagger, for that was short; but look on God's finger in Ehud's hand, and that can work wonders. Look not on the ordinance, but on the Ordainer; [not] on the means, but on the Means-maker: neither be offended at the meanness of the one, but admire the majesty of the other.

USE.

It confutes the Papists, who, displeased, as it were, at the simplicity of the sacraments, as God hath instituted them, seek to better and amend them by their own additions. Thus they account plain water in baptism too mean; and therefore they mingle it with cream, oil, spittle, and other ingredients, which I as little know what they be, as they know why they use them. Yea, all their service of God is not only made sweet, but luscious to the palate of flesh; and they plainly show by their baits what fish they angle to catch; namely, rather to get men's senses than their souls, and their eyes than their judgments.

Not that I am displeased with neatness, or plead for nastiness, in God's service. Surely God would have the Church, His Spouse, as not a harlot, so not a slut; and, indeed, outward decency in the church is a harbinger to provide a lodging for inward devotion to follow after. But we would not have religion so bedaubed with lace that one cannot see the cloth; and ceremonies which should adorn, obscure the substance of the sacraments, and God's worship. And let us labour to be men in Christianity, and not only like little children to go to school, to look on the gilt and gaudy babies of our books, and to be allured to God's service by the outward pomp and splendour of it. But let us love Religion, not for her clothes, but for her face; and then shall we affect it, if she should chance (as God forbid) to be either naked through poverty, or ragged through persecution. In a word, if God hath appointed it, let us love the plainness of His ordinance, though therein there be neither warm water, nor strong water, nor sweet water, but plain water of Jordan.

Come we now to the *quoties*, "how often." He dipped himself seven times; that is, he went in, and washed himself, and came out again; and went in, and washed himself, and came out again; and so till the seventh time. Thou, therefore, whosoever thou art, who art afflicted in body or mind, or any other way, do not grudge against God, and grieve in thyself, if thy pain be not eased in an instant, if thy malady be not removed in a moment. O tarry the Lord's leisure; (the Lord's pleasure is the Lord's leisure;) wait and attend His time. Think not that thou shalt not be cured at all, because thou art not all cured at once. Naaman himself was not completely cleansed at the first entrance into Jordan, but it cost him seven times' washing.

The number of seven is most remarkable in Holy Writ, and passeth for the emblem of perfection or completeness; as well it may, consisting of an unity in the middle, guarded and attended with a trinity on either side. Once, I must confess, I find this number of seven to be defective and too little; and yet the correction and supplying thereof still runs on a septenary number: " Shall I forgive my brother seven times?" " Yea," said our Saviour, " seventy seven times." If any ask, why God pitched on this number, and imposed [it] on Naaman; the best answer I can make shall be in the words of our Saviour, Matthew xi. 26: " Even so, Father; because it pleased Thee well." Naaman was bid to wash seven times, and he did wash seven times. Hence observe,

DOCTRINE.

We must observe God's commandments, both in matter and manner, both in substance and circumstance. But some will say, " Had Naaman washed once more or less, under or over seven times, would so small a matter have broken any squares? and would God have imposed any penalty on so slight a forfeiture?" I answer, Things that are small in themselves swell great, when they are either forbidden or commanded by God. Look upon Lot's wife, looking back with carnal eyes, and it will seem a small offence. O how flesh and blood could easily be her advocate, to plead for her! What if she did look back? She did no more, and could do no less, and be a mother. Would you have her to be a pillar of stone, before she was a pillar of salt? I mean, so hard, so remorseless, as not to send one farewell glance to that unfortunate city, wherein she had so much kindred and acquaintance? Well, however, we must know, the offence was most heinous, by the heaviness of the punishment inflicted upon her.

And as it is thus in small things forbidden, so is it in small things commanded. They must be precisely observed. In those general maps of the world which are usually made in a sheet of paper, the least prick or point which can be made with a pen extends to five miles at the least: but I say, the smallest deviation and declination, the least imaginable deflection, from the commanded will of God, is an infinite distance from it, as breaking the command of an infinite God, and deserveth infinite punishment.

Observe, therefore, not only all things considerable, but *all* things in God's will: for, indeed, all things therein are considerable; not only every syllable, but every iota, the least letter; yea, every prick, comma, and accent, hath his emphasis, and must be pronounced in our practice. As Moses, therefore, in making the tabernacle, made it in all things alike to the pattern he saw in the mount, not a knop, or a bowl, or an almond, in the candlestick, under or over; not a bell, or a pomegranate, in Aaron's coat, more or less; but *concordat copia cum originali*, the transcript agreed with the original in all things: so let us precisely follow the instructions God giveth us. Let us not willingly be heteroclites from His will; either defectives, to do too little, or redundants, to do too much: but let us be truly regular; not washing more than seven times, with the superstitious man; nor less than seven times, with the profane man; but, with Naaman in my text, just seven times.

When I compare our present occasion with this history we have treated of, I find a great resemblance betwixt them. Here is a little child to be cured of a leprosy. For so may original corruption fitly be called,—First, for the hereditariness of it: it is a successive disease, entailed from father to child, ever since the fall of our first parent Adam. Secondly, from the over-spreading nature thereof; the infection defiling all the powers of our souls, and parts of our bodies. Here also is the water of Jordan to wash it away. Since Christ washed Jordan by being washed in it, He hath given it a power to cleanse our original corruption. Some thieves have eat off their irons, and fretted off their fetters, with mercury water; but there is no way to work off the chains of our natural corruption,—whereby our feet are hurt in the stocks, the irons have entered into our souls,—but only by the water in baptism. Only the maidenhead and virginity of the water, in the pool of Bethesda, was medicinal to cure diseases: he that came first was cured; the second got no profit. But in our Jordan, our water in the font, the virtue thereof is not lessened in the using; the child that is last baptized shall receive as much benefit as that which is first washed therein.

But herein, I must confess, there is a difference on the cure of Naaman and this child: he was totally and perfectly cleansed from his leprosy; but this child is washed but in part, so far as is God's pleasure. The condemning power of original corruption is drowned in the font; but, though the bane be removed, the blot doth remain; the guilt is remitted, the blemish is retained; the sting is gone, the stain doth stay; which, if not consented to, cannot damn this infant, though it may hereafter defile it. Secondly, the final peaceable-commanding* power

* [This is evidently a misprint; but it is difficult to conjecture precisely what the author wrote here. *Peaceable* should, perhaps, be *peccable*; the meaning being, that the dominant power of corruption in

A CHRISTENING SERMON. 183

is washed away in the laver of regeneration; though afterwards it may dwell in us, it shall no domineer over us; it may remain there as a slave, not as a sovereign, sure not as a lawful one, be he ever resisted, often subdued, though never expelled. These things deserve larger prosecution; but this is none of Joshua's day, wherein the sun standeth still; and therefore I must conclude with the time.

our nature is washed away in regeneration. The latter part of the sentence also seems incorrect; *be he* being probably an error for *but be.*—ED.]

FACTION CONFUTED.

1 COR. I. 12:

Now this I say, that every one of you saith, I am of Paul; and I am of Apollos; and I am of Cephas; and I am of Christ.

SUCH is the subtilty of Satan, and such is the frailty of the flesh, though things be ordered never so well, they will quickly decline. Luther was wont to say, he never knew a good order last above fifteen years. This speedy decaying of goodness you may see in the church of Corinth, from which St. Paul was no sooner departed, but they departed from his doctrine. Some, more carried by fancy than ruled by reason, or more swayed by carnal reason than governed by grace, made choice of some particular pastor, whom they extolled, to the great disgrace of his fellow ministers, and greater dishonour of God Himself. Now St. Paul, "not willing to make" these ministers "a public example," concealeth their persons, yet discovereth the fault; and, making bold with his brethren, Apollos and Cephas, applieth to them and himself what the Corinthians spake of their fancied preachers. "Now this I say, that every one of you saith, I am of Paul; and I am of Apollos; and I am of Cephas; and I am of Christ."

OBJECTION.

But the apostle herein hath made no good choice, to mention Cephas: for he was only known to the Corinthians by his fame, not by his person; seeing it appears not, either in Scripture or ecclesiastical story, that ever Cephas (that is, St. Peter) was ever at Corinth.

ANSWER.

This hinders not the application of the apostle, granting St. Peter was never there; for many ministers are most admired at distance,—*Major è longinquo reverentia :* * like some kind of stuff, they have the best gloss a good way off; more than "a prophet in his own country." Thus the good esteem which foreigners have conceived of the piety and learning of the Geneva ministers, hath been the best stake in the hedge of that state.

I need not divide the words, which in themselves are nothing else but division, and contain four sorts of people, like the four sorts of seed, Matthew xiii.;—the three first bad; the last

* Tacitus.

only, "I am of Christ," being good and commendable.

"I am of Paul:" as if they had said, "There is a preacher called Paul; his matter is so powerful, his method so pleasing, his doctrine so sound, his life so sincere; his preaching I affect, or his person I prefer; 'I am of Paul.'" "Tush," saith another, "what talk you of Paul? Indeed, his epistles are powerful and strong; but his bodily presence is weak, and his speech of none effect. There is one Apollos, an eloquent man, and mighty in the Scriptures; he stands highest in my esteem; 'I am of Apollos.'" "Fie," saith a third, "why name you Apollos,—one that learnt the best part of his divinity from Aquila and Priscilla, a layman and a weak woman? There is one Cephas, that caught three hundred souls at the preaching of one sermon; that is the man for my money: I will say of him, as Gehazi did of Naaman, 'As the Lord liveth, I will run after him.' 'I am of Cephas.'" "Well," saith a fourth, "Paul I know, and Apollos I know, and Cephas I know; men endowed with great grace, and eminent instruments of God's glory: I acknowledge them as the channel, but God alone as the Fountain, of faith and conversion; and do attend on Him alone in these His instruments; 'I am of Christ.'"

DOCTRINE.

The staple doctrine herein to be observed is this: *The factious affecting one pastor above another is very dangerous.* Indeed, we may, and must, give a famous part of reverence, and a Benjamin's portion of respect, to those who, *datâ paritate in ceteris*, excel in age, pains, parts, and piety. 1. In age; for he is a traitor against the crown of old age, who payeth not the allegiance of respect due thereunto. Such reverence the hoary hairs of Gousartius did deserve, when for more than fifty years he had been a preacher in Geneva. 2. In pains; being such as have borne the heat of the day; so that the stress of the ministry hath lain heaviest on their shoulders. Such an elder is "worthy of double honour." 3. In parts; being stars of the first magnitude, brightly shining with their rich endowments. 4. In piety; which setteth a lustre on all the former. But the factious affecting of ministers, lavishing *by wholesale* all honour on one, and scarce *retaliating* out any respect to the other,—raising high rampires to the praise of the one, by digging deep ditches to discredit and disgrace another,—is that which St. Paul doth reprove in my text, and we must confute at this time.

Four great mischiefs will arise from this practice.

MISCHIEF I.

First, it will set enmity and dissension betwixt the ministers of God's word.

I confess, we that either have or intend to take on us the high calling and holy function of the clergy, ought to endeavour, by God's grace, so to qualify ourselves, that our affections never mistake the true object, nor exceed their due measure. But, alas! such is our misery (rather to be bemoaned than amended; the perfect removing whereof is more to be desired than hoped for) that as long as we carry corruption about us, we are men "subject to like passion with" others. Hence is it come to pass that, as the Grecians (Acts vi. 1) murmured against the Hebrews, " because their widows were neglected in the daily ministration ; " so ministers will find themselves aggrieved, that people, in the partial dispensing of their respect, pass them by unregarded. Perchance the matter may fly so high as it did betwixt Moses and Aaron, Numbers xii. 2: " And they said, Hath the Lord indeed spoken only by Moses? Hath he not spoken also by us ? " It will anger not only Saul, a mere carnal man, but even those that have degrees of grace: " He hath converted his thousands, but such a one his ten thousands." These discords betwixt ministers, I could as heartily wish they were false, as I do certainly know they are too true.

MISCHIEF' II.

It will set dissension amongst people, whilst they violently engage their affections for their pastors. The woman that pleaded before Solomon, (1 Kings iii. 22,) "The living child is mine," said she, "but this dead child is thine." "Nay," said the other, "but thy son is dead, and my son is the living." Thus will they fall out about their pastors. "The living minister is mine; he that hath life, spirit, and activity, in the manner and matter of his delivery: but the dead minister is thine; flash in his matter, confused in his method, dreaming in his utterance. He cometh not to the quick; he toucheth not the conscience; at the most, with Joash, king of Israel, (2 Kings xiii. 18,) he smites the Aramites but thrice,— leaves off reproving a vice before people be fully reformed." "Nay," saith the other, "my minister is the living minister, and thine is the dead one. Thy pastor is like the fire, 1 Kings xix. 12; flashing in the flames of ill tempered and undiscreet zeal; 'but the Lord was not in the fire:' or like the earthquake, shaking his auditors with ill applied terrors of the law; 'but the Lord was not in the earthquake:' whilst my minister is like to a 'still voice;' and the Lord was in the still voice; stanching the bleeding-hearted penitent, and dropping the oil of the Gospel into the wounded conscience."

MISCHIEF III.

It will give just occasion to wicked men to rejoice at these dissensions, to whose ears our discords are the sweetest harmony. O, then, let not the herdsmen of Abraham and Lot fall out, whilst the Canaanites and Perizzites are yet in the land. Let not us dissent, whilst many adversaries of the truth are mingled amongst us, who will make sport thereat.

MISCHIEF IV.

Lastly, it will cause great dishonour to God Himself; His ordinance in the mean time being neglected. Here is such doting on the dish, there is no regarding the dainties; such looking on the ambassador, there is no notice taken of the King that sent him. Even Mary's complaint is now verified: "They have taken away the Lord, and placed Him I know not where." And as, in times of Popery, Thomas Becket dispossessed our Saviour of His church in Canterbury; (instead of Christ's Church, being called St. Thomas' Church;) and whereas rich oblations were made to the shrine of that supposed saint, *summo altari nil*, nothing was offered to Christ at the communion table; so, whilst some sacrifice the reverence to this admired preacher, and others almost adore this affected pastor, God in His ordinance is neglected, and the word, being the savour of life, is had in respect of persons.

To prevent these mischiefs, both pastors and people must lend their helping hands. I begin with the pastors; and first with those whose churches are crowded with the thickest audience.

Let them not pride themselves with the bubble of popular applause, often as causelessly gotten as undeservedly lost. Have we not seen those who have preferred the onions and fleshpots of Egypt before heavenly manna, lungs before brains, and sounding of a voice before soundness of matter? Well, let princes count the credit of their kingdoms to consist in the multitude of their subjects: far be it from a preacher to glory when his congregation swells to a tympany, by the consumption of the audience of his neighbour minister.

Yea, when pastors perceive people transported with an immoderate admiration of them, let them labour to confute them in their groundless humours. When St. John would have worshipped the angel, "See thou do it not," saith he: "worship God." So, when people post headlong in affecting their pastors, they ought to wave and decline this popular honour, and to seek to transmit and fasten it on the God of heaven. Christ went into the wilderness, when the people would have made Him a king: let us shun, yea, fly such dangerous honour, and tear off our heads such wreaths as people would tie upon them; striving rather to throw mists and clouds of privacy on ourselves, than to affect a shining appearance. But know, whosoever thou art, who herein art an epicure, and lovest to glut thyself with people's applause, thou shalt surfeit of it before thy death; it shall prove at the last pricks in thy eyes, and thorns in thy side,—a great affliction, if not a ruin, unto thee; because sacrilegiously thou hast robbed God of His honour.

Let them labour also to ingratiate every pastor, who hath tolerability of desert, with his own congregation. It was the boon Saul begged of Samuel, "Honour me before my people." And surely it is but reason we should seek to grace the shepherd in the presence of his flock: though perchance privately we may reprove him, disgrace him not publicly before those that are under him.

I am come now to neglected ministers, at whose churches *solitudo ante ostium,* and within them too, whilst others, perchance less deserving, are more frequented.

Let not such grieve in themselves, or repine at their brethren. When St. John Baptist's disciples told him that all flocked to Jesus, whom he baptized beyond Jordan; "I must decrease," answered he, "and He must increase." Never fret thyself, or vex out thy soul, if others be preferred before thee. They have their time; they are crescents in their waxing, full seas in their flowing: envy not at their prosperity. " The stars in their course did fight against Sisera;" thy course of credit may chance to be next, thy turn of honour may chance to come after. One told a Grecian statist, who had excellently deserved of the city he lived in, that the city had chosen four-and-twenty officers, and yet left him out. "I am glad," said he, "the city affords twenty-four abler than myself." So let ministers triumph and rejoice in this, that the church yields so many men better meriting than themselves, and be far from taking exception thereat.

And let us practise St. Paul's precept, "by honour and dishonour, by good report and disreport." "Seven years have I served God in good esteem, and well respected; by the time I have served God so long in disgrace and reproach, perchance the circulation of my credit may return, and with patience I may regain the esteem I have lost;" and if otherwise, let him say with David, "Lord, here I am; do with Thy servant as Thou pleasest."

By this time, methinks, I hear the people saying unto me, as the soldiers to John Baptist, "But what shall we do?" Now the counsel I commend to you is this.

REMEDY I.

First, ever preserve a reverent esteem of the minister whom God hath placed over thee. For, if a sparrow lighteth not on the ground without

God's especial providence, surely no minister is bestowed in any parish without a more immediate and peculiar disposing of God; and surely their own pastor is best acquainted with their diseases, and therefore best knoweth to apply spiritual physic thereunto. And as God's word hath a general blessing on every place, so more particularly is it sanctified and blessed there, to those parishioners, from the mouth of their lawful minister. Let not therefore the sermon of a stranger, who perchance makes a feast of set purpose to entertain new guests, be preferred before the pains of thy own minister, who keeps a constant house and a set table, each Lord's Day, feeding his own family. Wherefore, let all the Ephesians confine themselves to their Timothy; Cretians to their Titus; every congregation to their proper pastor. And I hope pastors, considering the solemn oath they took at their institution, and the profit they receive from their people, and how irrational it is to take wages and do no work, and the heavy account they must make at the day of judgment, will provide milk in their breasts for those who must suck of them. As for those whose necessary occasions do command their absence from their flocks, let them be curates of their curates,—oversee such whom they appoint to oversee their people. Columella gives this counsel to husbandmen: "Never keep a horse to do that work which may be done by an ass;" both because asses are of a lower price, and cheaper kept. But God forbid ministers should observe this rule, and so consult with their profit as to provide unworthy substitutes, to save charges.

REMEDY II.

Let them not make odious comparisons betwixt ministers of eminent parts. It is said of Hezekiah, 2 Kings xviii. 5, that "after him was none like him, of all the kings of Judah, neither any that were before him." It is said also of King Josiah, 2 Kings xxiii. 25, "And like unto him there was no king before him, that turned to the Lord with all his heart, and with all his soul, and with all his might; neither after him rose up any like him." The Holy Spirit prefers neither for better, but concludes both for best; and so amongst ministers, when each differs from others, all may be excellent in their kinds. As, in comparing several handsome persons, one surpasseth for the beauty of a naturally painted face; a second, for the feature of a well proportioned body; a third, for a grace of gesture and comeliness of carriage; so that Justice itself may be puzzled, and forced to suspend her verdict, not knowing where to adjudge the victory: so may it be betwixt several pastors. One's excellency may consist in the unsnarling of a known controversy;

another, in plain expounding of Scripture, to make it portable in the weakest memory: one, the best Boanerges; another, the best Barnabas: our judgments may be best informed by one, our affections moved by a second, our lives reformed by a third. I am persuaded there is no minister in England, for his endowments, like Saul, "higher than his brethren from the shoulders upwards;" but rather some hundreds like the pillars in Solomon's house, all of a height. But grant some in parts far inferior to others: was not Abishai a valiant and worthy captain, though he attained not to the honour of the first three?' And may not many be serviceable in the church, though not to be ranked in the first form, for their sufficiency?

Let them entertain this for a certain truth, that the efficacy of God's word depends not on the parts of the minister, but on God's blessing, on His ordinance. Indeed, there is a generation of preachers that come upon the stage before ever they were in the tiring-house,—whose backwardness in the university makes them so forward in the country; where what they lack in learning, they supply in boldness. I could wish, that as when Hagar's tle of water was spent, God opened her eyes, and she went to the fountain again; (Gen. xxi. 19;) so, when these novices have emptied their store of set sermons they brought with them, that their parents would remit them back to the university, the fountain of learning and religion, to furnish themselves with a better stock of sufficiency. Such ministers as these I account as none at all : but as for those that have the *minimum ut sic*, the least degree of tolerability, to enable them in some measure to discharge their office, God may be, and often is, as effectual in and by them as by rabbis of far greater parts.

To conclude : let us, with one mind and one mouth, advance the glory of God, that thereby the Gospel may be graced ; wicked men amazed,— some of them converted, the rest of them confounded ; weak Christians confirmed ; to the grief of devils, joy of angels, honour of God Himself. Amen.

FINIS.

DAVID'S { HEINOUS SIN.
　　　　　　HEARTY REPENTANCE.
　　　　　　HEAVY PUNISHMENT.

EXODUS xxxv. 23.
AND every man, with whom was found goats' hair, and red skins of rams, and badgers' skins, brought them [to the building of the Tabernacle].

AD ZOILUM.
Thy lays thou utt'rest not, yet carpest mine;
Carp mine no longer, or else utter thine.

By THOMAS FULLER,
MASTER OF ARTS, OF SIDNEY COLLEGE IN CAMBRIDGE.

LONDON:
PRINTED BY THO. COTES, FOR JOHN BELLAMIE,
DWELLING AT THE THREE GOLDEN LIONS IN CORNHILL.
1631.

TO THE HONOURABLE MR. EDWARD, MR. WILLIAM,
AND MR. CHRISTOPHER MONTAGU, SONS TO THE
RIGHT HONOURABLE EDWARD LORD MONTAGU, OF
BOUGHTON.

FAIR branches of a stock as fair,
Each a son, and each an heir;
Two *Joseph*-like, from sire so sage
Sprung in autumn of his age;
But a *Benjamin* the other,
Gain'd with losing of his mother!
This fruit of some spare hours I spent
To your Honours I present.

A king I for my subject have,
And noble patrons well may crave.
Things tripartite are fit for three;
With youths, things youthful best agree.
Take them therefore in good part,
Of him that ever prayeth in heart
That as in height ye wax apace,
Your souls may higher grow in grace:

Whilst your father (like the green
Eagle in his scutcheon seen,
Which with bill his age doth cast)
May longer still and longer last;
To see your virtues o'er-increase
Your years, ere he departs in peace.
Thus I my book, to make an end,
To you, and you to God, commend.
  Your Honours' in all service,
    THO. FULLER.

DAVID'S HEINOUS SIN.

1.

How Zion's Psalmist grievously offended,
How Israel's Harper did most foully slide,
Yet how that Psalmist penitent amended,
And how that Harper patient did abide
    Deserved chastisement; (so fitly styled,
    Which wrath inflicted not, but love most mild,
    Not for to hurt, but heal a wanton child;)

2.

How one by her own brother was defiled;
And how that brother by a brother slain;
And how a father by his son exiled,
And by a subject how a sovereign;
    How peace procured after battles fierce,
    As *Sol* at length doth sullen clouds disperse;
    My Muse intends the subject of her verse.

3.

Great God of might, whose power most sovereign
Depends of none, yet all of Thee depend!
Time cannot measure, neither place contain,
Nor wit of man Thy being comprehend:
   For whilst I think on Three, I am confined
   To One; and when I One conceive in mind,
   I am recall'd to Three, in One combined.

4.

Thy help I crave, thy furtherance I ask;
My head, my heart, my hand direct and guide,
That, whilst I undertake this weighty task,
I from thy written lore start not aside.
   Alas! 'tis nothing, Lord, with Thee to break
   The strong; 'tis nothing to support the weak,
   To make men dumb, to make an infant speak.

5.

Each one begotten by immortal seed,
Becomes the pitch'd field of two deadly foes,
Spirit and Flesh: these never are agreed,
With truceless war each other doth oppose;
   And though the Spirit oft the Flesh doth quell,
   It may subdue, but can it not expel,
   So stoutly doth the Jebusite rebel.

6.

Now David, when on Bathsheba loose eyes
He fix'd, his heavenly half did him dissuade:
"Turn, turn away thy sight from vanities;
Exchange thy object; else thou wilt be made
  Unmindful of thy soul, her corps * to mind;
  Made for to lose the truth, such toys to find;
  By looking long, made at the last stark blind.

7.

"What though her face and body be most fair?
Behold, the sun her beauty doth surpass;
His golden beams surmount her yellow hair
As far as purest crystal dirty glass:
  Her skin, as is the sky, not half so clear;
  Her curious veins for colour come not near
  Those azure streaks that in the heavens appear.

8.

"There let thy hungry sight her famine feed,
Whereon it cannot surfeit with excess:
Whilst tongue, heart, harp, are tuned up with speed,
The grand Contriver's glory to express;
  Framing with words, to raise His mighty name,
  That with a mighty word did raise this frame,
  And by His providence preserves the same.

* [Fuller frequently uses this word simply in the sense of *body*,— not *dead body*,—and sometimes treats it as a *plural* noun.—ED.]

9.

"But let no lustful thoughts lodge in thy mind;
Before that they be born, they must be kill'd;
Or else the man is cruel that is kind,
To spare the foes wherewith his soul is spill'd:
 And if a wanton motion may request
 Leave for to lodge a limb, th' encroaching guest
 Will soon command room to receive the rest.

10.

"Look towards the midday sun, and thou shalt see
A little tower * o'er tops of hills to peep;
That is the birth-place of thy pedigree;
Full oft there hast thou fed thy father's sheep,
 And kept his flocks upon the flowery plain.
 But now the sheep-hook of a country swain
 Is turn'd the sceptre of a sovereign.

11.

"God made thee great; O, do not Him disgrace,
And by His weighty statutes lightly set.
He honour'd thee; O, do not Him debase:
He thee remember'd; do not Him forget.
 Why should fat Jeshurun † so wanton grow
 As at his Master's head his heels to throw?
 Master, that all his feeding did bestow.

* The tower of Eder, nigh Bethlehem, seven miles from Jerusalem.
† Deut. xxxvii. 15.

12.

"Behold high cedars in the valley set;
They in thy eyes like little shrubs do show,
Whilst little shrubs upon Mount Olivet
Seem lofty cedars. Men whose states are low,
   Their sins are not so obvious to sense.
   In princes, persons of great eminence,
   A smaller fault doth seem a great offence.

13.

"But grant no man thy wickedness espies;
Surely the Searcher of the reins doth mark
Even infant lust: can fig-leaves blear His eyes?
Or can thy shame be shrouded in the dark?
   Darkness shall then be turned into light;
   Yes, darkness is no darkness in His sight,
   But seem the same to Him both day and night."

14.

The Spirit had resolved more to speak,
But her half-spoken words the Flesh confounds.
Nor wonder is it she, so used to break
God's laws, not passing for to pass their bounds,
   Against man's rules of manners should offend;
   Which now, impatient longer to attend,
   Began before her rival made an end.

15.

" If ever Nature lavishly did throw
Her gifts on one, which might have served more,
Yet make them comely; if she e'er did show
The prime, and pride, and plenty of her store;
 Lo, there's the form wherein she hath express'd
 Her utmost power, and done the very best,
 Her master-piece surpassing all the rest.

16.

" What if those careless tresses were attired?
Sure, then her face for comeliness transcends;
What now seems lovely, then would be admired,
If Art might but begin where Nature ends.
 Alas! ten thousand pities 't is indeed
 That princes on so common fare should feed,
 Whilst common men on princely meat exceed.

17.

" Always the same doth glut the appetite,
But pleased is our palate with exchange;
Variety of dishes doth delight:
Then give thy loose affections leave to range.
 Forbidden things are best; and when we eat
 What we have slily gotten by deceit,
 Those morsels only make the dainty meat."

18.

But, O, reserve thyself, my maiden Muse,
For a more modest subject, and forbear
To tune such wanton toys as may abuse
And give distaste unto a virgin's ear.
    Such rotten reasons first from hell did flow,
    And thither let the same in silence go,
  Best known of them that did them never know.

19.

Thus he that conquer'd men, and beast most cruel,
(Whose greedy paws with felon goods were found,)
Answer'd Goliath's challenge in a duel,
And laid the giant grovelling on the ground;
    He, that of Philistines two hundred slew,
    No whit appalled at their grisly hue;
  Him one frail woman's beauty did subdue.

20.

Man is a ship, affections the sail,
The world the sea, our sins the rocks and shelves;
God is the Pilot: if He please to fail,
And leave the steering of us to ourselves,
    Against the ragged rocks we run amain,
    Or else the winding shelves do us detain,
  Till God, the Palinure, returns again.

P

21.

Yet David, bold to sin, did fear the shame;
He shunn'd the sheath, that ran upon the knife;
With a fine fetch providing for his fame,
He fetcheth home Uriah to his wife :
  So, under his chaste love, to cloak his own
  Unlawful lust, to fault most careless grown,
  Most careful that his fault should not be known.

22.

But in their plots God doth befool the wise,
By ways that none can trace, all must admire :
Short of his house that night Uriah lies,
And David so came short of his desire :
  The man a nearer lodging-place did use,
  (Which made the king on further plots to muse,)
  And, sent home, home to go did thus refuse :

23.

"The pilgrim ark doth sojourn in a tent;
In open fields Joab my lord doth lie,
And all the soldiers of his regiment
Have earth their beds, the heaven their canopy,
  Where bitter blasts of stormy winds are rife :
  Shall I go feast, drink, dally with my wife?
  Not, as I live, and by your lordship's life."

24.

Then by his servants David did conspire,
Uriah's lust so dull with wine to edge:
(Venus doth freeze, where Bacchus yields no fire:)
By their constraint, he condescends to pledge
    One common cup that was begun to all
    Captains encamped nigh to Rabba wall;
    One specially, unto the general.

25.

Abishai next is drunk to, Joab's brother;
And this cup to a second paves the way,
That orderly doth usher in another:
Thus wine, once walking, knows not where to stay.
    Yea, such a course methodical they take
    In ordering of cups, the same did make
    Uriah quite all order to forsake.

26.

His false supporters soon begin to slip;
And if his faltering tongue doth chance to light
On some long word, he speedily doth clip
The train thereof: yea, his deceitful sight
    All objects paired doth present to him;
    As double faces, both obscure and dim,
    Seem in a lying looking-glass to swim.

27.

My prayers for friends' prosperity and wealth
Shall ne'er be wanting; but if I refuse
To hurt myself by drinking others' health,
O, let ingenuous natures me excuse.
   If men bad manners this esteem, then I
   Desire to be esteem'd unmannerly,
     That, to live well, will suffer wine to die.

28.

Well did blind Homer see, for to express
This vice, that spawns all other; when he feigns
Dame Circe, an enchanting sorceress,
Whose cups made many men forego their brains;
   Whilst, with the witless ass, one purely doats,
   Others misshaped are, like lustful goats,
     Or swill-engrossing swine, with greedy throats.

29.

Though bad, yet better was Uriah left;
Not quite a beast, though scarce a man; disturb'd
In mind, but not distracted, nor bereft
Of wit; though drunk, yet soberly he curb'd
   His lust, being wise, though ignorant, to cross
   The king's designs, who now new thoughts
     doth toss,
   Finding his former project at a loss.

30.

The Night with mourning weeds the world beclad,
When restless David, for to mend his matter,
Did make it worse : his naked sin was bad,
More monstrous being mask'd : they oft do scatter
    The chain, that of God's laws unloose a link.
    He swam before in sin, nigh to the brink;
    But now he means in midst thereof to sink.

31.

Then for a light he speedily did call,
(Thou, Darkness, with his project best agreed,)
For paper, pen, and ink, to write withal;
Though, sure, a poniard might have done the deed
    Better, if he in blood had dipped it;
    And on a sheet of paper what he writ,
    A winding-sheet far better did befit.

32.

This, certs, I know, as sepian juice did sink
Into his spongy paper, sabling o'er
The same with various-formed specks of ink,
Which was so pure and lily-white before;
    So spots of sin the writer's soul did stain,
    Whose soily tincture did therein remain,
    Till brinish tears had wash'd it out again.

33.

Next day, when Day was scarce an infant grown,
Uriah, (that no mischief did mistrust,
As none he did deserve, but by his own
Did measure all men's dealings to be just,)
    Bearing this letter, on his journey pass'd
    With speed, who needed not to make such haste,
    Whose death, had he gone slow, did come too fast.

34.

Thus crafty masters, when they mind to beat
A careless boy, to gather birch they send him;
The little lad doth make the rod complete,
Thinking his master therefore will commend him:
    But, busily employ'd, he little thought
    He made the net wherein himself was caught,
    And must be beaten with the birch he brought.

35.

His journey came well to the welcome end:
Safe to the Town of Waters * he attains;
Town which to force, Joab his force did bend;
(Nought is so hard but vincible by pains;)
    Some with their heads did plot, some with their hand
    Did practise; yes, as ready was the band
    To serve, as was the captain to command.

* Rabba, 2 Sam. xii. 27.

36.

So busy bees, some fly abroad at large,
Of flowery nectar for to fetch their fill;
Some stay at home, for to receive their charge,
And trustily the liquor do distil,
   Or bottle it in wax; whilst others strive,
   Like sturdy marshals, far away to drive
The drowsy drones that harbour in the hive.

37.

The strong-arm'd archer, from his crooked bow,
Made a straight shaft, with dismal news to speed
Into the town, which ne'er return'd to show
The sender how his message did succeed:
   Yea, heavy bodies mounted were on high;
   Dull stones, to which Dame Nature did deny
Feet for to go, Art made them wings to fly.

38.

Whilst in the town one with his friend did talk,
A sudden stroke did take his tongue away;
Some had their legs arrested, as they walk,
By martial law, commanding them to stay:
   Here falls a massy beam, a mighty wall
   Comes tumbling there, and many men doth maul,
Who were both slain and buried by the fall.

39.

Were there not used, in the days of yore,
Enough men-murdering engines, but our age,
Witty in wickedness, must make them more,
By new-found plots, men's malice to enrage?
   So that fire-spitting cannons, to the cost
   Of Christian blood, all valour have engross'd,
   Whose finding makes that many a life is lost.

40.

Whilst thus the well appointed army sought,
Winding in worm-like trenches near the wall,
To humble the proud towers, Uriah brought
The speaking paper to the general;
   Who, when such language he therein did find,
   He thought himself or else the king was blind,
   Himself in body, or the king in mind.

41.

Then he the letter did peruse again:
The words the words of David could not be;
And yet the hand, for David's hand was plain;
He thought it was, and thought it was not, he:
   Each little line he thoroughly did view,
   Till at the length more credulous he grew,
   And what he thought was false, he found too true.

42.

Now Joab, let thy valour be display'd;
Act not a midwife to a deed unjust;
By fear or favour be not oversway'd
To prove a pander to a prince's lust:
   Return a humble answer back again,
   Let each word breathe submission, to obtain
   By prayers a conquest of thy sovereign.

43.

Show how, when God and country's good requires,
Then substance, soul, and body to engage
Is the ambition of thy best desires:
Foes foreign to resist, to quell their rage,
   How willingly wouldst thou thyself despise,
   Count losing of thy goods a gainful prize,
   Lavish thy blood, and thy life sacrifice!

44.

But when God's love directly doth withstand,
And where His laws the contrary convince,
We must not break the heavenly King's command,
Whilst we do seek to please an earthly prince.
   The burdens they impose on us to bear,
   Our duty is to suffer them; but where
   Kings bid, and God forbids, we must forbear.

45.

Behold, the man, whose valour once surmounted
In sacking Zion's mount, (mount not so high
As men therein were haughty,) and accounted
Of worthies chief, doth most unworthily:
   He that to sum the people of the land
   Withstood the king, now with the king doth stand
   Too buxom for to finish his command.

46.

Next morn, when early Phœbus first arose,
(Which then arose last in Uriah's sight,)
Him Joab in the forefront did dispose,
From whom the rest recoiled in the fight.
   Thus of his friends betray'd by subtil train,
   Assaulted of his foes with might and main,
   He lost his life, not conquered, but slain.

47.

His mangled body they expose to scorn;
And now each craven coward dare defy him,
Outstaring his pale visage, which beforne
Were palsy-struck, with trembling to come nigh him.
   Thus heartless hares with purblind eyes do peer
   In the dead lion's paws; yea, dastard deer
   Over his breathless corps dare domineer.

DAVID'S HEARTY REPENTANCE.

1.

The tongue of guiltless blood is never tied
In the earth's mouth; and though the greedy
ground
Her gaping crannies quickly did provide,
To drink the liquor of Uriah's wound,
   Yet it with moans bescattered the skies,
   And the revoicing Echo with replies
Did descant on the plain-song of the cries.

2.

Hereat the Lord, perceiving how the field
He sow'd with grace, and compass'd with a heap
Of many mercies, store of sins did yield,
Where He expected store of thanks to reap,—
   With flames of anger furnace-like He burn'd;
   For patience long despised and lewdly spurn'd
Is at the length to raging fury turn'd.

3.

Then all the creatures mustered their train,
From angels unto worms; the blind did see
Their Lord disgraced, whose honour to maintain
Things wanting life most lively seem to be;
  Refusing all to serve man, that refused
  To serve his God; all striving to be used
  To punish him, his Maker that abused.

4.

" Please it your Highness for to give me leave,
I'll scorch the wretch to cinders," said the Fire:
" Send me," said Air; " him I'll of breath
    bereave : "
" No," quoth the earnest Water, " I desire
  His soily sins with deluges to scour : "
" Nay, let my Lord," quoth Earth, " employ
    my power;
With yawning chaps I will him quick devour."

5.

Soon with a word the Lord appeased this strife,
Enjoining silence, till He did unfold
That precious volume, call'd the Book of Life,
Which He the Printer, privileged of old,
  Containing those He freely did embrace;
  Nor ever would I wish a higher grace
  Than in this Book to have the lowest place.

6.

Within this Book he sought for David's name ;
Which having found, he proffered to blot.
(And David surely well deserved the same,
That did his nature so with sin bespot ;
  Though none are blotted out but such as never
  Were written in ; nothing God's love can sever ;
  Once written there, are written there for ever.)

7.

Straight from His throne the Prince of Peace arose,
And with embraces did His Father bind ;
Imprisoning His arms, He did so close,
As loving ivy on an oak did wind,
  And with her curling flexures it betrail :
  His Father, glad to find His force to fail,
  Struggled, as one not willing to prevail.

8.

Thus, then, began the spotless Lamb to speak
(One word of whom would rend the sturdy rock,
Make hammer-scorning adamant to break,
And unto sense persuade the senseless stock :
  Yea, God Himself, that knows not to repent,
  Is made by His petitions penitent,
  His justice made with mercy to relent) :

9.

" Why doth My Father's fury burn so fierce?
Shall *Persian* laws unalterable stand?
And shall My Lord decree and then reverse,
Enact and then repeal, and countermand?
   Tender Thy credit, gracious God, I crave,
   And kill not him thou didst conclude to save:
   Can these hands blot what these hands did engrave?

10.

" Hath not Thy wisdom, from eternity,
Before the world's foundation first was laid,
Decreed, the due time once expired, that I
Should flesh become, and Man born of a maid;
   To live in poverty, and die with pain;
   That so Thy Son, for sinners vilely slain,
   Might make vile sinners be Thy sons again?

11.

" Let Me, O let Me thy fierce wrath assuage,
And for this sinner beg a full discharge.
What though he justly doth provoke Thy rage?
Thy justice I will satisfy at large.
   If that the Lord of life must murder'd be,
   Let me entreat this murderer may go free,
   My merits cast on him, his sins on Me."

12.

Thus speaking, from His fragrant clothes there went
A pleasant breath, whose odour did excel
Myrrh, aloes, and cassia for scent,
And all perfumed His Father with the smell;
  Whereat His smoothed face most sweetly smiled,
  And, hugging in His arms His dearest Child,
  Return'd these welcome words with voice most mild:

13.

"Who can so pleasing violence withstand?
Thy craving is the having a request;
Such mild entreaties do My heart command,
The amends is made, and pacified I rest:
  As far as earth from heaven does distant lie,
  As east is parted from the western sky,
  So far his sins are sever'd from Mine eye."

14.

Hereat the heavenly choir lift up their voice,
Angels and saints imparadised combine,
Upon their golden viols, to rejoice,
To raise the praise of the celestial Trine:
  All in their songs a sacred strife express'd,
  Which should sing better, and surpass the rest:
  All did surpass themselves, and sang the best.

15.

Then said the Fire, "My fury I recant;
Life-hatching warmth I will for him provide:"
"If David's breathless lungs do chance to pant,"
Said Air, "I'll fan them with a windy tide:"
"With moisture I'll," said Water, "quench
    his heat:"
"And I his hunger," quoth the Earth, "with meat,
Of marrow, fatness, and the flower of wheat."

16.

Thus when a lord, long buried in disgrace,
A king to former favour doth restore,
With all respect the court doth him embrace,
Fawning as fast as they did flout before:
    Whose smiles, or frowns, are but the bare re-
      flection
    Of the king's face, and like to this direction,—
    Where he affects, they settle their affection.

17.

Plain-dealing Nathan presently was sent;
Nathan, than whom was none more skill'd to
    lanch [lance]
A fester'd soul, and with a searching tent
To sound the sore; more cunning none to stanch
    A bleeding-hearted sinner, nor more kind,
    With swaddling clothes of comfort, for to bind
    Unjointed members of a troubled mind.

18.

He did not flow with wealth, which envy breeds,
Nor yet was he with penury oppress'd :
Want is the cause from which contempt proceeds :
His means were in the mean, and that's the best.
   High hills are parch'd with heat, or hid with snow ;
   And humble dales soon drown'd, that lie too low ;
   Whilst happy grain on hanging hills doth grow.

19.

For sundry duties he did days divide,
Making exchange of work his recreation :
For prayer he set the precious morn aside,
The midday he bequeath'd to meditation ;
   Sweet sacred stories he reserved for night ;
   To read of Moses' meekness, Samson's might,
   These were his joy, these only his delight.

20.

But now dispensing with his daily task,
To court he comes, and wisely did invent,
Under a parable, his mind to mask,
Seeming to mean nought less than what he meant ;
   And, lapwing-like, round fluttering a while,
   With far-fetch'd preface and a witty wile,
   He made the king himself for to beguile.

21.

Thus he that thought all mortal men to cheat,
And with false shows his secret sins to shade,
Was cozen'd by the innocent deceit
Of one plain prophet, and directly made,
   As he a judge sate on the bench, to stand
   At bar a prisoner, holding up his hand,*
   But first condemned by his own command.†

22.

Go, fond affecters of a flaunting strain,
Whose sermons strike at sins with slanting blows;
Give me the man that's powerful and plain,
The monster Vice unmasked to expose.
   Such preachers do the soul and marrow part,
   And cause the guilty conscience to smart;
   Such please no itching ears, but pierce the heart.

23.

This made King David's marble mind to melt,
And to the former temper to return,
Thawing his frozen breast, whenas he felt
The lively sparks of grace therein to burn,
   Which under ashes cold were choked before;
   And now he weeps, and wails, and sighs full sore,
   Though sure such sorrow did his joy restore.

---

* "Thou art the man."
† "The man that hath done this thing shall die."

24.

So have I seen one slumber'd in a swound,
Whose sullen soul into his heart did hie;
His pensive friends soon heave him from the
 ground,
And to his face life water do apply:
  At length, a long-expected sigh doth strive
  To bring the welcome news, "The man's alive,"
  Whose soul at last doth in each part arrive.

25.

Then to his harp he did himself betake,
(His tongue-tied harp, long grown out of request,)
And next to this his glory must awake,
The member he of all accounted best.
  Then, with those hands which he for grief did
    wring,
  He also lightly strikes the warbling string,
  And makes one voice serve both to sob and sing.

26.

That heavenly voice to hear I more desire,
Than Syren's sweetest songs; than music made
By Philomele, chief of the winged choir;
Or him, whose lays so pleasing did persuade
  Stones for to lackey, when he went before;
  Or that brave harper, whom unto the shore
  His hackney dolphin safely did restore.

DAVID'S HEAVY PUNISHMENT.

1.

Most true it is, when penitents by grace
Acquitted are, the pardon of their sins,
And punishment's release, do both embrace,
Like to a pair of undivided twins;
   Parted they cannot be, they cleave so fast:
   Yet, when the tempest of God's wrath is past,.
   Still His afflicting honey-shower doth last.

2.

But let the Schools these thorny points dispute,
Whose searching sight can naked Truth descry
Skulking in Error's arms, and are acute,
Fine-finger'd with distinctions to untie
   Knots more than Gordian: these men never miss'd
   The slender mark, like those * in whose left fist
   There did so much dexterity consist.

        * Judges xx. 16.

3.

Meantime, my Muse, come see how prettily
The patient infant doth itself behave;
Infant but newly born, now near to die,*
That from the cradle posted to the grave.
    See with what silent signs, and sighs full fain,
    Poor heart! it would express where lies the pain,
    Complaining that it knows not to complain.

4.

Stay, cruel Death, thy hand for pity hold;
Against some aged grandsire bend thy bow,
That now hath full twice forty winters told,
Whose head is silver'd o'er with age's snow:
    Dash out this babe out of thy dismal bill,
    And in exchange let him thy number fill;
    So may he live, his friends enjoy him still.

5.

Those hands to hurt another never sought,
Which cannot help themselves, they are so weak;
His heart did never hatch a wanton thought;
His tongue did never lie, that cannot speak:
    By wrong and violence he ne'er did wrest
    The goods wherewith his neighbour was possess'd,
    Whose strength scarce serves to suck his nurse's breast.

* The death of King David's child.

6.

But, ah! this infant's guilt from him proceeds,
That knew the least, when most he sought to
 know;
Who was most naked, when clothed in his weeds;
Best clothed then, when naked he did go.
  In vain the wit of wisest men doth strive
  To cut off this entail, that doth derive
  Death unto all, when first they are alive.

7.

As when a tender rose begins to blow,
Yet scarce unswaddled is, some wanton maid,
Pleased with the smell, allured with the show,
Will not reprieve it till it hath display'd
  The folded leaves, but to her breast applies
  The abortive bud, where coffined it lies,
  Losing the blushing dye before it dies.

8.

So this babe's life, newly begun, did end,
Which sure received the substance, though not
 sign'd
With grace's seal: God freely doth attend
His ordinance, but will not be confined
  Thereto, when 't's not neglected, nor despised:
  They that want *water* are by *fire* baptized;
  Those sanctified, that ne'er were circumcised.

9.

Sweet babe! one Sabbath thou on earth didst see,
But endless Sabbaths dost in heaven survive.
Grant, Death of joyful hours deprived thee;
Thou hadst seen years of sorrows, if alive.
 True, thou wert born a prince, but now [thou] art
 A king by death: sleep therefore in the ground
 Sweetly, until the trumpet last shall sound.

10.

By this child's death, King David did sustain
One loss; but where this misery did end,
More miseries began; as in a chain
One link doth on another link depend:
 His lust with lust, his slaying with a slaughter,
 Must punish'd be: proportioned thereafter,
 To mother Sin is Punishment the daughter.

11.

Amnon, advised by Jonadab, a fit
Of sickness feigns: men wickedly inclined
Worse counsellors (that with great store of wit
Have dearth of grace) most easily may find;
 And Tamar's hands his meat must only make.*
 Ah, happy age! when ladies learnt to bake,
 And when kings' daughters knew to knead a cake!

* The deflowering of Tamar.

12.

Rebekah was esteem'd of comely hue,
Yet not so nice her comeliness to keep,
But that she water for the camels drew:
Rachel was fair, yet fed her father's sheep.
   But now, for to supply Rebekah's place,
   Or do as Rachel did, is counted base;
   Our dainty dames would take it in disgrace.

13.

But quickly did his beastly lust declare,
That he to eat her dainties had no need;
He for the cook, not for the cates, did care;
She was the dish on whom he meant to feed.
   O, how she pray'd, and strove with might and main!
   And then from striving fell to prayers again;
   But prayers and striving both alike in vain.

14.

Thus a poor lark, imprison'd in the cage
Of a kite's claws, most sweetly sings at large
Her own dirge, whilst she seeks to calm his rage,
And from her jailer sues for a discharge;
   Who, passing for no music that surpass'd,
   To feed his ears, whilst that his guts do fast,
   On her that pray'd so long, doth prey at last.

15.

Then with dust-powder'd hair she sore bewails,
And punish'd on herself, her brother's sin,
Parting her maiden livery with nails,
That parted was with colours, and wherein
 White streaks their owner's innocence did show;
 The bashful *red* her modesty : the row
 Of *sable* sorrow'd for the wearer's woe.

16.

Comfort thyself, more virtuous than fair,
More fair than happy virgin! mourn with measure;
Sins unconsented to no souls impair,
That must be done perchance with body's pleasure,
 Which with the grief of soul may be constrain'd;
 The casket broke, the jewel still remain'd,
 Untouch'd, which in the casket was contain'd.

17.

In his breast Absalom * records this wrong :
Out of our minds good turns do quickly pass,
But injuries therein remain too long;
Those scrawl'd in dust, but these engraved in brass.
 One sunset for our anger should suffice;
 Which in his wrath set oft, oft did arise,
 With yearly race surrounding twice the skies.

   * The murdering of Amnon.

18.

Now when his fruitful flocks, which long had worn
Their woollen coats, for to make others hot,
Were now to forfeit them, and to be shorn,
(Sure from the silly sheep his devilish plot
  Their owner never learnt,) he finds a way
  To work revenge, and called on that day
  His brothers to a feast, which proved a fray.

19.

What Amnon drunk in wine, in blood he spilt,
Which did the dainties mar, and meat defile;
Cups, carpets, all with gory streaks were gilt,
Seeming to blush, that cruelty so vile,
  So foully savage, should the banquet stain:
  Thus he that, being well, did sickness feign,
  Not being sick, was on a sudden slain.

20.

The rest refused on the meal to feed,
Whose bellies were so full with grief and fear
To feel what they have seen; away they speed
To ride, but Fame did fly, Fame that doth wear
  A hundred listening ears, a hundred eyes,
  A hundred prating tongues; she daily plies
  Tongues that both tell the truth and tattle lies.

21.

She gets by going, and doth gather strength,
As balls of snow by rolling more do gain;
She whisper'd first, but loudly blazed at length,
" All the king's sons, all the king's sons are slain!"
   The pensive court in doleful dumps did rue
   This dismal case, till they the matter knew:
   Would all bad news, like this, might prove untrue!

22.

Go, silly souls, that do so much admire
Court-curious entertainment and fine fare:
May you, for one, obtain what you desire;
I for your fowls of Phasis * do not care,
   If that such riots at your feasts be rife,
   And all your meat so sourly sauced with strife,
   That guests, to pay the shot, must lose their life.

23.

Happy those swains that in some shady bower,
Making the grass their cloth, the ground their board,
Do feed on mellow fruit, or milk's fine flower,
Using no wine but what their wells afford:
   At these did Malice never bend her bow;
   Their state is shot-free, it is set so low,
   They overlook that would them overthrow.

---

* [Pheasants; reputed to have been first imported into Greece from the banks of the Phasis.—ED.]

24.

Fast unto Geshur flies the fratricide,
To shelter there himself; the sentence sore
Of angry Justice fearing to abide.
O happy turn, had he return'd no more!
   Who wonted guise kept in a country strange:
   Those that abroad to foreign parts do range,
   Their climate, not conditions, do exchange.

25.

Return'd, at entrance of the court he stands; *
If any suitors there he chanced to find,
He steals their hearts by taking of their hands,
And sucked out their soul with kisses kind:
   He of their name, cause, city doth inquire.
   Proud men prove base, to compass their desire;
   They lowest crouch, that highest do aspire.

26.

Before such kisses come upon my face,
O, let the deadly scorpion me sting:
Yea, rather than such arms should me embrace,
Let curling snakes about my body cling:
   Than such fair words I'd rather hear the foul
   Untuned screeching of the doleful owl,
   Or hear the direful mountain wolf to howl.

* Absalom's aspiring to the kingdom.

27.

Some men affirm that Absalom doth sound
In the world's oldest tongue, " of peace a father :"
But certs I know that such mistake their ground ;
" Rebellious son," sure, it importeth rather.
   And yet why so ? sith since I call to mind,
   Than the *Clementes* none were more unkind,
   Than *Innocent* more nocent none I find.

28.

Then, borrowing the plausible disguise
Of holiness, he mask'd his plot so evil
Under the good pretence of sacrifice.
(A saint dissembled is a double devil.)
   But sure were these the vows he went to pay;
   His sire, that harmless sheep, he vow'd to slay,
   Who o'er Mount Olives weeping fled away.

29.

This makes me call my Saviour's grief to mind,
Who on this mount,* because the Jews were grown
So wicked,—those that said they saw, so blind,—
Mourn'd for their sins, that mourn'd not for their
   own :
   Much did He weep for others, that forbad
   Others to weep for Him, whose being sad
   Hath made His saints, for ever since, full glad.

      * Luke xix. 42.

30.

Down comes the king to Jordan : on the sand
If that the sailors chance to ground the boat,
A flood of tears they straightways did command,
Whose large accession made the vessel float;
   And if a blast of wind did chance to fail,
   So grievously the people did bewail,
   Their very sighs might serve to stuff the sail.

31.

Thus was the king in his own land exiled;
His subjects were his host, and he their guest,
Whose place was ill supplied by his child,
(Unhappy bird, defiling his own nest!)
   That took his father's wives in open sight :
   Those that do want of grace the sunshine bright,
   Extinguish oft dim nature's candle-light.

32.

The blushing Sun no sooner did behold
So beastly lust, but sought his face to shroud,
And, shrinking in his beams of burnish'd gold,
Was glad to skulk within a sullen cloud :
   The shamefaced birds, with one wing fain to fly,
   Did hold their other fan before their eye,
   For fear they should such filthiness espy.

33.

What needed he, to keep alive his name,
Erect a pillar ? Sure, this damned deed
Makes us remember and detest the same,
That in the world's last doting age succeed :
   Yea, when that brass, that seemeth time to scorn,
   Shall be by all-devouring time outworn,
   His name they'll bear in mind that are not born.

34.

But he that gave this counsel did not speed ; *
Who, speeding home on witless ass amain,
(Ass that, for wit, his rider did exceed,)
'Cause he his will at court could not obtain,
   Did make his will at home : the peevish elf
   Amongst his household parts his cursed pelf,
   Careful of that, but careless of himself.

35.

O, sudden thought of thy mortality !
Thou art not yet so thorough worn with age,
None in thy face such symptoms can espy,
Which should so near approaching death presage :
   Thy state is not distempered with heat ;
   Thy working pulse doth moderately beat ;
   All outward things seem whole, seem all complete :

---

* Ahithophel hanging himself.

36.

But ghostly is thy grief: thou that by treason
Against thy liege so lately wast combined,
Thy passions now rebel against thy reason,
Reason, that is the sovereign of thy mind,
   And seek for to disturb it from the throne.
   Strive, strive to set these civil broils at one;
   Order thyself, and let thy house alone.

37.

A chain of hemp he to his neck made fast,
By tying of which knot he did untie
The knot of soul and body, and at last,
Stopping the passage of his breath, thereby
   A passage for his soul wide open'd he.
   Thus traitors, rather than they should go free,
   Themselves the hangmen of themselves will be.

38.

His friends to balm his body spare no cost,
With spices seeking to perfume a sink:
For certs I know, their labour was but lost;
His rotten memory will ever stink;
   His soul thereby was nothing bettered,
   Because his corps were bravely buried;
   Tombs please the living, profit not the dead.

39.

How many worthy martyrs, vilely slain,
Made meat for fowls, or for the fire made fuel!
Though ground they could not for a grave obtain,
Were not less happy, but their foes more cruel:
   Unburied bodies made not them unblest;
   Their better half did find a heavenly rest,
And doth enjoy joys not to be express'd.

40.

Leave we the traitor thus, upon whose hearse
My muse shall not a precious tear misspend;
Proceeding to bemoan in doleful verse,
How two great bands with cruel blows contend;*
   Whole clouds of arrows made the sky to lower,
   Dissolved at length into a bloody shower,
Till steel kill'd many, wood did more devour.

41.

O, let it not be publish'd in the path
That leads unto the incestuous seed of Lot;
Tell not these tidings in the town of Gath,
In Ascalon see ye proclaim it not,
   Lest these rejoice at this calamity,
   Who count your fame their greatest infamy,
Your woful jar their welcome melody.

* The battle betwixt Absalom and David's men.

42.

Had Rachel now revived, her sons to see,
Their bloody hands would make her heart to bleed;
Each a Benoni unto her would be.
Had Leah lived to see herself agreed
  To fall out with herself, with tears, most sure,
  She would have made her tender eyes past cure:
  Whoever won, she must the loss endure.

43.

The conquest, which her verdict long suspended,
Hover'd aloft, not knowing where to light;
But at the last the lesser side befriended
With best success; the other put to flight;
  More trusted a swift foot than a strong fist.
  Most voices oft of verity have miss'd,
  Nor in most men doth victory consist.

44.

The graceless son was plunged in deep distress;
For earth his weight no longer would endure;
The angry heavens denied all access
Unto a wretch so wicked, so impure:
  At last the heavens and earth, with one consent,
  A middle place unto the monster lent,
  Above the earth, beneath the firmament.

45.

His skittish mule ran roving in the fields,
And up high hills, down dales, o'er woods did
    prance,
Seeming with neighing noise, and wanton heels,
In token of great joy to sing and dance,
    That now her master she should bear no more,
    (A heavy bulk, whose sins did weigh so sore,)
    Now rid of him that rid on her before.

46.

Cry, Absalom, cry, Absalom, amain,
And let thy winged prayers pierce the sky;
O, to the Spring of pity soon complain,
That ne'er is dammed up, nor drained dry;
    Thy fault confess, His favour eke implore;
    Much is thy misery, His mercy more;
    Thy want is great, but greater is His store.

47.

Condemn thyself, and He shall thee acquit;
Do thou but pray, He'll pity thy estate;
Confess thy debt, He will the same remit;
It never was too soon, it's ne'er too late.
    Alas! long sinners scarce at last relent:
    He gives not all offenders to repent,
    That granteth pardon to all penitent.

48.

Whilst thus his life suspended was on high,
Bold-venturous Joab opened his heart,
(Heart, where much treason lurked privily,)
And pierced his body with a triple dart:
   Then crimson blades of grass, whereon he bleeds,
   Did straightways die, and in their room succeeds
   A fruitful wilderness, of fruitless weeds.

49.

When David heard the victory was gain'd,
But his son lost, (as Jordan, waxing rank,
O'erflows the land, and scorns to be restrain'd,
To have his tide tied in a narrow bank,)
   Surges of sorrow in his heart did rise,
   And break the watery sluices of his eyes,
   Who lighten'd thus himself with heavy cries:

50.

" My son, whose body had of grace the fill,
My son, whose soul was so devoid of grace;
Without my knowledge, and against my will,
My son, in cause so bad, so strange a place!
   My son, my son,—for which I most complain,—
   I fear, in soul, as in the body, slain!
   Would I might die, that thou might'st live
     again!"

51.

Now when this grief was swallow'd, not digested,
The subjects flock'd, king David to restore,
Who in an instant love what they detested,
Detest in th' instant what they loved before.
   People, like weathercocks, waved with the wind,
   We constant in unconstancy may find;
   As time counts minutes, so they change their mind.

52.

Amongst the rest, that came the king to meet,
Lame-legg'd Mephibosheth, but loyal-hearted,
Was one, that never wash'd his clothes or feet,
(Except with tears,) since David first departed;
   Feet, which by fall from nurse's arms began
   To halt; with him a child so fast she ran,
   That he could never go, when grown a man.

53.

Not much unlike, if it give no distaste
That real truths I do with trifles match,
Whilst that my posting Muse with headlong haste
Doth strive her rural lays for to dispatch,
   Halting invention, for the want of heed,
   And lame unjointed lines from her proceed,
   And seldom things done speedily do speed.

54.

But here an unexpected jar arose,
Whilst people for most part in prince contended;
Which grew from bitter words to bloody blows.
"The king," quoth Judah, "of our tribe
    descended;
  He of our flesh is flesh, bone of our bone."
"Nay," answer'd Israel, "in the king we own
Ten parts; a single share is yours alone."

55.

Whilst sparks of discord thus began to smoke,
To find the bellows, Sheba did conspire,
(Sheba* that proudly did disdain the yoke,)
And, blowing of a trumpet, blew the fire.
  Then those that claimed ten, disdain'd all part
  In David; taught by his seducing art,
  They discontented to their tents depart.

56.

This rebel Joab whilst to quell he strives,
A nameless woman (in the book of life
Her name is kept, that kept so many lives)
Procured that he who stirred up the strife,
  The body of the commonwealth to rend
  From prince the head, whereon it did depend,
  With head from body rent, his life did end.

* The son of Belial.

57.

By his death many citizens survived;
The loss of traitor's blood did prove their gain;
Soon ceased the flood of discord, thence derived,
When they the factious fountain did restrain.
  This war a vile man with a word * did raise,
  Unto his shame; which, to her endless praise,
  A worthy woman with a word † allays.

58.

So, in our land, a noble queen arose,
As we have heard our fathers oft relate;
A maid, yet manly to confound her foes,
A maid, and yet a mother to the state:
  Which she weak, like to crumbling brick, did find,
  Which strong as lasting marble she resign'd;
  Gold and God's worship both by her refined.

59.

She, having flourished in great renown,
In spite of power and policy of Spain,
Did change her earthly for a heavenly crown,
And ceased to rule o'er men, with God to reign.
  Forty and four Novembers fully past,
  (Ay me, that winged time should post so fast!)
  To Christ, her Love, she wedded was at last.

---

* " What part have we in David," &c.
† " His head shall be thrown," &c.

60.

This sun thus set, there followed no night
In our horizon; straight another sun
Most happily continued the light
Which by the first was hopefully begun:
    And, what might most amaze all mortal eyes,
    Never before out of the northern skies
    Did men behold bright Phœbus to arise.

61.

Arts did increase his fame; he did increase
The fame of arts; and, counting twice eleven
Twelvemonths upon his throne, this prince of peace,
By falling to the earth, did rise to heaven.
    Then down our cheeks tears hot and cold did flow;
    Those for the sire deceased express'd our woe,
    Those joy for his succeeding son did show.

62.

Live, gracious liege, whose virtues do surmount
All flattery, and Envy them admires;
Centre of grace and greatness, live to count
Till that thy kingdom with the world expires.
    We subjects wish thee worst, that love thee best,
    Who here long to enjoy thee do request,
    That late thou mayst enjoy a heavenly rest.

63.

And thou, young prince, hope of the future age,
Succeed to father's virtues, name, and crown.
A new star did thy Saviour's birth presage,
His death the sun eclipsed did renown:
  But both of these conjoined to adorn
  Thy welcome birth; the sun, with age so worn,
  Did seem half dead, and a young star was born.

64.

But what dost thou, my venturous Muse, presume
So far above thy dwarf-like strength to strain?
Such soaring soon will melt thy waxen plume.
Let those heroic sparks, whose learned brain
  Doth merit chaplets of victorious bays,
  Make kings the subjects of their lofty lays:
  Thy worthless praising doth their worth dispraise.

65.

Strike sail, and to thy matter draw more near,
And draw thy matter nearer to an end;
Though nought praiseworthy in thy verse appear,
Yet strive that shortness may the same commend.
  Return to see where Joab homeward goes,
  To see his friends, that had subdued his foes;
  His soldiers and himself there to repose.

66.

Thus, when two adverse winds, with strong command,
Summon the sea, the waves, that both do feel,
Dare follow neither, but in doubt do stand;
Whilst that the ships, with water drunk, do reel
   With men, for grief of drowning, drown'd in grief;
   Until at length a calm brings them relief,
   And stills the storm, that had so long been brief.

67.

O that I might but live to see the day,
(Day that I more desire than hope to see,)
When, all these bloody discords done away,
Our princes in like manner might agree;
   When all the world might smile in perfect peace,
   And these long-lasting broils at length might cease,
   Broils which, alas! do daily more increase!

68.

The Netherlands with endless wars are toss'd,
Like in success to their unconstant tide,
Losing their gettings, gaining what they lost:
Denmark both sword and Baltic seas divide:

More blood than juice of grape nigh Rhine is
    shed;
And Brunswick land will not be comforted,
But cries, "My duke, alas! my duke is dead."

69.

The wars in France, now laid aside, not ended,
Are only skinned over with a scar;
Yea, haughty Alps, that to the clouds ascended,
Are over-climbed with a bloody war:
    And Maro's birthplace, Mantua, is more
    Made famous now for Mars, and battle sore,
    Than for his Muse it famed was before.

70.

Sweden to stop the imperial flood provides;
(May his good cause be crown'd with like success;
And they, that now please none, to please both
    sides,
May they themselves his trusty friends express!)
    But Turks the cobweb of their truce each hour
    Do break; they wait a time, but want no power,
    Nor will,war-wearied Christians to devour.

DAVID'S HEAVY PUNISHMENT.

71.

But let the cunning CHYMIC, whose exact
Skill caused light from darkness to proceed,
Out of disorder order can extract,
Make in His due time all these jars agreed,
 Whose grievances may be bemoan'd by men,
 By God alone redressed: and till then
 They more befit my prayers than my pen.

ΤΩ ΜΟΝΩ ΔΟΞΑ ΘΕΩ.

FINIS.

LONDON:
PRINTED BY WILLIAM NICHOLS,
46, HOXTON SQUARE.

www.ingramcontent.com/pod-product-compliance
Lightning Source LLC
Chambersburg PA
CBHW021350230426
43666CB00006B/475